Instant Memory Training for Success

Practical techniques for a sharper mind

Chester Santos

CAPSTONE
A Wiley Brand

This edition first published 2016
© 2016 Chester Santos

Registered office
John Wiley & Sons Ltd, The Atrium, Southern Gate, Chichester, West Sussex,
PO19 8SQ, United Kingdom

For details of our global editorial offices, for customer services and for
information about how to apply for permission to reuse the copyright material
in this book please see our website at www.wiley.com.

Library of Congress Cataloging-in-Publication Data is available

A catalogue record for this book is available from the British Library.

ISBN 978-0-857-08706-5 (pbk)
ISBN 978-0-857-08708-9 (ebk) ISBN 978-0-857-08711-9 (ebk)

Cover Design: Wiley
Hand drawn type: © Giorgio Morara/Shutterstock

Set in 12/14pt SabonLTStd by Aptara Inc., New Delhi, India
Printed in Great Britain by TJ International Ltd, Padstow, Cornwall, UK

Contents

Introduction

Over the course of the last decade, I've appeared on various television shows demonstrating what many people have called "extraordinary" feats of memory. Some things that I've managed to memorize include: the exact order of a shuffled deck of playing cards in under two minutes; a computer generated random sequence of 100+ digits forwards and backwards in five minutes; the names of more than 200 people in an audience after having heard each name only one time; all Kentucky Derby results since its inception in 1875, and more than 4000 pieces of data about all 535 members of the United States Congress including each congressperson's first name, last name, state, district number, political party, all congressional committees on which they serve, and more. I did also manage to win the USA Memory Championship, which required me to successfully pull off some of the feats that I just described as well as many more. However, I want to emphasize that there is nothing different or *special* about my brain compared to that of the average person. The superpower memory that I've developed is the result of *training* and *practice*. *You* are also capable of doing extraordinary things with your memory, and this can help you to be more successful in your career and personal life!

Since becoming a memory champion, I've dedicated my life to helping other people to unlock the extraordinary power of their minds. With this book, I will teach you some *simple* and *fun* techniques to help you to easily remember names, speeches and presentations, important facts and figures, foreign languages, course material, and much more! Drawing on almost a decade of experience teaching memory techniques to people from all over the world, I've included in this book techniques that are not only the most powerful and effective but also the easiest for *anyone* to learn.

This is not a book about the very broad topic of human memory. There are many aspects to memory and a lot of brain science that you won't find included. This is also not a *comprehensive* book about memory training. I've purposely omitted various techniques that I'm aware of and have personally used, because I feel they are not a good fit for this particular book. You are holding in your hands what I believe to be one of the simplest and most straightforward *introductions* to memory training ever written. This is a short book with information that is easy to digest and put into practice right away. In a matter of days or less, you will be able to enjoy impressing your friends, colleagues, and clients with your new memory abilities.

One of the most rewarding aspects of my career has been the privilege of seeing people light up and become giddy with excitement once they realize how much they are truly capable of remembering. Unlike at my live speeches and seminars, I won't be able to see your face, but it is my sincere hope that this book provides you with that type of excitement. Cheers to your success!

Chester Santos
"The International Man of Memory"

1

Overview: Your Most Valuable Business Asset

What is your most valuable business asset? Leadership, sales, or communication skills? Is it your creativity or ability to reason? Maybe it's your ability to network and develop relationships? Guess again. What is the *one thing* that has the biggest influence on your ability to succeed? I'll give you a clue. It's at the very *core* of all those things. Your brain is what determines your ability to acquire and develop any and *all* new skills, so it follows that the most valuable business asset that you possess is the power of your own brain!

To date, there is no supercomputer in the world that comes close to even a fraction of the processing power of the human brain. Your brain possesses a number of absolutely incredible abilities that are just waiting to be fully realized. One of these abilities is that of a *super power memory*, and with this book I am going to help you unlock this incredible power within you. You will soon be able to remember just about anything quickly, easily, and with tremendous accuracy!

Whether you're an executive, entrepreneur, small business owner, other professional, or newly graduated student about to enter the business world, you can benefit greatly from improving your ability to remember. In this age of Google and Wikipedia, with people perhaps becoming a little too dependent on apps to do their remembering for them, being able to actually remember things yourself will set you apart and demonstrate true knowledge and expertise. As the rest of the business world loses its ability to remember, your superpower memory will become even more valuable.

We all want to hire and do business with those professionals that we perceive to be the *experts* in their particular fields. Let's say you're unfortunately in need of an attorney to sort out an unpleasant situation you're faced with. You first talk with an attorney named Eye Phonie. After listening to you describe your case, Eye says that he's sure he can help you, but that he'll need to do some research and get back to you with recommendations. You ask him about a couple of cases that you read about while doing some research of your own, and also about a few statutes that you think may be relevant when arguing your case. Eye says that he *thinks* he's heard of those cases but would have to look them up. He also says that he'll need to *brush up* on the statutes. Eye seems like a capable attorney, but you aren't particularly impressed.

You next talk with an attorney named Mem Ory. Upon hearing the facts of your case, Mem is able to talk from memory about prior cases similar to yours and how those cases played out. He also cites relevant statutes that are going to be important when arguing your case. Mem hits on everything you discovered in your own research and much more. You immediately think to yourself that this guy is clearly an expert! He's definitely the attorney you'd like to hire. Recalling important information during his meeting with you allowed Mem to demonstrate his knowledge and expertise. When you still need to look everything up, you come off as more of a student or novice as opposed to an expert.

*   *   *

Two marketing firms are competing for a certain corporation's business. The representative from the firm called WeNeedNotes gives her presentation first. She pulls up a slide, reads it to the corporation's board, then pulls up another slide and does the same thing. Her whole presentation basically consists of reading slide after slide to the board members. Unfortunately, the pretty pictures and fancy graphs aren't enough to keep some of the corporation's board members from dozing off. After the WeNeedNotes rep leaves, the corporation's board members talk about how they could have just read the presentation themselves at home.

The next day it's time for the representative from NoteLess to give her presentation. She has no slides or notes, and instead conducts her presentation entirely from memory. The board members are very impressed with her knowledge about the corporation in general, the challenges it faces, and how NoteLess can address their corporation's marketing needs. By giving a presentation without notes, the NoteLess rep is able to keep the board awake and engaged while at the same time demonstrating impressive knowledge. This is one marketing contract that WeNeedNotes will not get!

There are two companies with very similar products and services. One is run by a CEO named Ifor Geta. He's known as being very forgetful. It's common for him to completely blank out on the names of people that have worked for the company for many years. Even worse he often calls employees by the wrong name! His presentation skills are lacking, so he has someone write presentations for him and then simply reads the slides. He is not quite up to speed on the latest technologies and trends in his company's industry, because things change quickly and he doesn't have the time to learn everything. The morale at Ifor's company is low and its employees are feeling less than inspired by their leader. Ifor isn't a bad guy. He just finds it difficult to remember things.

A totally different work environment exists at a company run by Ifor's competitor, Irem Ember. Irem is incredibly popular with his employees. He remembers all of their names, the names of their family members, and also their personal interests.

His employees really *feel* that he cares. They are also incredibly impressed with their CEO and they are inspired by him. His presentation skills, knowledge, and expertise are legendary! All of Irem's employees swear that his ability to remember is like a *super power*, and that Irem himself is like a *super hero*! The morale at Irem's company is very high and his employees feel very lucky to work for him. Which executive would you rather be?

* * *

There are two candidates interviewing for the same job. Their names are John Forget and Steve Remember. John and Steve's résumés are almost identical in terms of education, skills, and work experience. During John's interview he is quizzed a bit on some of the skills listed on his résumé. John doesn't do too well and tells the interviewer that he's been trained in that skill but that it's been a while and that he'll need to review it. The interviewer asks John a question about one of the company's most popular product offerings and John demonstrates that he clearly isn't familiar with the product. In fact, before the interview, John had read about that product and some others that the company offers, but he just can't recall the information confidently during the interview. John is asked what advantages the company offers over its competitors and although John has read about this, he's not able to give much of a response due to not being able to recall key details.

Fortunately for Steve, he's read *Instant Memory Training for Success* and has developed some powerful memory skills. So, the night before his interview, Steve reviews his resume and outlines all the major concepts from the skill areas listed on his resume. He researches the company he'll be interviewing with and lists 10 key advantages that the company offers over its competitors. Steve then researches the company's products and outlines exactly what the most popular products do. Next, Steve activates his *super power* and commits all of the information to memory in less than an hour! During Steve's interview, the interviewer is absolutely astonished with Steve's knowledge and expertise. Moreover, due to his razor sharp memory, Steve is *perceived* to be very *intelligent*, and who wouldn't want to hire the candidate that we think is the most intelligent? If you ever find yourself looking for a job, you really owe it to yourself to develop memory skills!

* * *

There are two politicians running against each other for office. The first politician is very experienced and well educated in the issues facing his potential constituents. However, when attending fundraisers, he finds it difficult to connect with potential donors to his campaign. His logic and reasoning are understood by the fundraiser attendees but he fails to move them and *connect* with them enough to the point that they *feel* compelled to open their wallets and donate to his campaign. The second politician makes everyone at his fundraiser fall in love with him by calling everyone by name, asking about their families, and talking about their personal interests as well as things that they have in common with him. He uses his carefully-honed memory skills to charm all of the attendees to the point that they are donating much more to his campaign than he was even hoping for. When a politician enters a room, he or she wants to know everything there is to know about everyone in that room! Politicians, perhaps more so than any other professionals, truly understand the power in remembering names and other things about people!

There are hundreds, if not thousands, of different groups and organizations dedicated to helping facilitate business networking. In fact, if done correctly, business networking can be one of the most cost-effective ways to grow a business. However, how many times have you run into someone whom you've previously met at a networking event only to have no clue what their name is or what they do for a living? If this is happening, then you really are not getting the most out of networking! You are losing out on opportunities to build better relationships with people!

Perhaps one day your company sends you to a series of expensive training sessions. When you return to your job after having gone through the training, you're unfortunately not able to recall much of what you were supposed to have learned. Your colleague, however, who went through the same training is able to recall everything and really excels in dealing with the new technologies and procedures. Whose career do you think will advance as the company transitions? You have in essence been left behind due to your inability to remember what you've learned!

* * *

In a city called Brainopolis, there are two renowned financial advisors. Both of them have had flourishing careers for decades. One of the advisors, named Learna Lot, has taken continuing education classes for years and about 10 years ago decided to develop memory skills and use them to learn as much as possible, including some foreign languages. As the years go by, Learna's mind remains razor sharp and her career flourishes all the way up until retirement. Unfortunately, the other advisor, named Electro Nic, became dependent on using electronic devices very early on in his career. He never used his memory because he felt it wasn't necessary when he could just have apps remember everything for him. During the last decade of his career, Electro's mental performance declined rapidly. He began to lose most of his clients and by the time retirement came around he could hardly even remember his own name!

Brain exercise has been a hot topic in recent years and it will continue to be a hot topic. Everyone is recommending a brain exercise programme nowadays in addition to a physical exercise programme. One of the best ways to exercise your brain is through memory training, and this can help keep you mentally sharp throughout your career!

I hope the potential scenarios I've described in this chapter have helped you realize that your most valuable business asset is your *brain*, and that one of the most important abilities to develop is your memory. Remembering can make your career, and forgetting can break it!

So, let's now start our journey together toward unlocking your super power memory!

2
The Building Blocks

In this chapter, you'll learn a number of techniques that will rapidly improve your memory. As a result of practising these techniques, you'll notice that as your memory improves, your concentration, imagination, creativity, and visualization ability will also improve. Developing these abilities is going to help you with multiple aspects of your career, and believe it or not, this training is going to be a lot of fun!

Improving your memory is actually very easy and fun to do. When going through the exercises in this chapter, just try to relax and have a good time. This isn't rocket science. In fact, you're going to be surprised at how easy it is. Learning to remember isn't hard work at all – instead, treat it just as a fun break from your regular daily routine. If you allow yourself to relax and enjoy yourself over the course of this chapter, then you'll be remembering not only more than you ever thought possible, but also *faster* than you ever thought possible. I'm going to help you tap into some of your hidden mental "super powers"! Are you ready? Let's go!

The Story Method

For your first exercise, we're going to work on using your imagination. The reason for this is because the ability to use your imagination is absolutely key to improving your memory. The better your imagination, the better your memory. You'll realize why that's true a little later on. I'm now going to guide you through a little scenario, and I just want you to try your best to "picture" what I describe. As you read my description, try to "see" it all happening in your mind. I'm not really much of a comedian, but I'll try my best to make you laugh. Let's use politicians for this, since they are almost always easy to make fun of. Which politicians to use? Well, how about Barack Obama from the United States and David Cameron from the United Kingdom? I'm sure you've seen your fair share of them on television over the years.

I want you to close your eyes and imagine that you walk into your residence and see Cameron and Obama standing in the middle of your living room. Yes, you read that correctly. David Cameron and Barack Obama are standing in the middle of your living room! Really try to visualize this. They are standing there behind podiums and are in the middle of a heated debate. You're completely shocked by what you're witnessing, but instead of asking any questions, you decide to just stand back and observe. This is not like any debate you've ever seen in your life. Not only is it happening right in the middle of your living room, but it is also the most heated debate you've ever witnessed.

You've actually never seen either one of them so angry before. Imagine what it would "feel" like to see this happening. They are sneering at each other, and all of a sudden you notice that Cameron is reaching behind his podium for something. Oh, wow! He's just taken out what appears to be a pie! He takes aim and sure enough … *splat!* The pie hits Obama square on target! You can see the pie running down Obama's face and he does not look happy at all. Believe it or not, you now see Obama reach behind his podium and also take out a pie. *Splat* again! Bull's eye! It seems Obama's aim is just as good as Cameron's, because the latter now has pie all over *his* face, too. In no time at all, a full-blown pie fight has broken out between the two! You can hardly believe what you are seeing, but right there in the middle of your living room, Cameron and Obama are battling it out in a pie fight!

Really try to picture this. See it happening in your mind. Have fun with it. Two prominent politicians from recent history are continuously throwing pies in each other's face! At this point, most likely you are experiencing some crazy visual images in your mind. Now, try to get even more of your senses involved. Imagine that in addition to seeing the pie fight happen, you can really "hear" it happening as well. You can hear the splattering of the pies as they hit each politician. *Splat! Splat!*

Now I want you to imagine something even more out of the ordinary. Imagine that you walk over to one of them and take some of the pie off his face. Imagine that you can "feel" the pie in your hands. Now imagine that you can even "smell" the pie. Imagine that it smells just like your favourite type of pie. Pumpkin? Cherry? Go ahead now and even "taste" some of the pie. *Mmmmm*, delicious!

At this point, please stop reading for a minute, close your eyes, and really experience that whole pie fight scenario happening in your mind as vividly as possible.

Go ahead. I'll wait ...

Okay. That exercise was pretty easy and fun, right? I hope it put a smile on your face. Well, I want you to know that if you were able to complete that exercise, then you have the ability to remember ANYTHING you want – quickly, easily, and for as long as you want! The reason for this is because your *visual memory* is the most powerful type of memory you have. Also, the more of your senses you can involve when encoding information, the easier it's going to be to retrieve that information later on.

Here's an example that illustrates the power of your visual memory. You've probably at some point in your life experienced a situation in which you saw someone you've met years in the past, recognized their face and knew that you had previously met them, but could not recall their name. Also, at some point, you've probably been asked questions about someone you've met years ago, and were able to call to mind at least a rough image of what the person looks like, but were not able to recall the name. This is because you've *seen* the person's face with your eyes, but you've never *seen* their name. Later on in this book, I'm going to teach you how to visualize and *see* a person's name, but for now I just want you to note the power of your *visual* memory.

I will now show you how to apply what you learned from the David Cameron and Barack Obama exercise to easily memorize a random list of words. The word list is as follows:

monkey

iron

rope

kite

house

paper

shoe

worm

envelope

pencil.

This random word list can easily be memorized, in order, by exercising your imagination as you did earlier. Close your eyes and go through the follow-ing process as I relate it:

I want you to imagine that you see a little mon-key dancing around. Really try to visualize him. Imagine that you can not only see the monkey, but you can also hear him making monkey sounds. You find yourself amused and chuckle as you observe his antics. While you're observing the monkey, all of a sudden you see him pick up a gigantic iron. Really try to visualize and experience this scenario in your mind. The little monkey somehow manages to pick up this gigantic iron and dances around with it. Eventually, the weight of the iron is too much and the iron begins to fall. As it falls, how-ever, a rope appears and attaches itself to the end of the iron.

You decide to walk over and feel the rope. Out of curiosity, you look up the rope, and see that it is attached to a kite. You reach up to try and touch the kite, but it's out of your reach. You watch as the kite flies around and crashes into the side of a house. This house, you notice, is for some strange reason completely covered in paper. You walk over to touch the paper, and as you do, a shoe magically appears and starts to walk all over the paper, causing it to move around. You notice that the shoe smells very bad. Wondering why the shoe is so smelly, you decide to take a look inside it. Inside the shoe, you see a worm crawling around. You feel disgusted as the worm crawls toward you, but it suddenly jumps out of the shoe and into an envelope. This envelope is unusual. It somehow manages to seal itself up. After you witness it being sealed, you see a pencil magically appear and begin to address the envelope.

Did you close your eyes and envision each little scenario? If not, re-read that paragraph and do so. Picture the dancing monkey... with the iron... attached to the rope... that holds a kite... that crashes into a house... etc. etc. etc.

Now, in order to recall the random word list, simply replay through the unusual and funny little story in your mind, starting with when you saw the monkey. As you do, simply take note of each major object that you encounter, and you will have recalled the random list of words in order: monkey, iron, rope, kite, house, paper, shoe, worm, envelope, pencil.

If you stumble at any point during the recall, quickly read the paragraph again. As you do, take special note to just relax and enjoy what you're seeing and experiencing in your mind. If you're smiling inwardly or outwardly while reviewing the scenario, that's a very good sign. Don't worry about having to remember anything. Just focus on vividly experiencing the scenario, and the remembering will come naturally!

This technique – of creating a vivid scenario or story in your mind to encode random information – is very powerful and easily extensible. What if the list were longer? For instance:

monkey

iron

rope

kite

house

paper

shoe

worm

envelope

pencil

river

rock

tree

cheese

coin.

After the pencil addresses the envelope, you could see it jump into a roaring river, the river crashes up against a rock, the rock smashes up against a tree, the tree has cheese in place of its leaves, and out of each piece of cheese falls a gigantic coin (pick your own denomination). Get the idea? Now close your eyes and do it again.

I'll wait …

You've just a learned a powerful technique that will help you to easily remember random bits of information, and at the same time exercise your creativity and imagination. This Story Method, as it is often called, primarily involves and exercises the right side of the brain. It's easy to work with and can be used in conjunction with the more advanced techniques we'll be learning later on. The more you practise using the story method to memorize information, the better you'll get at it. You'll begin to notice that you're able to create stories in your mind more quickly and experience them more vividly. At the end of this chapter, I've provided you with a number of word lists with which to practise.

The Body Method

We will now move on to learning a technique that will allow you to utilize *both* sides of your brain when encoding information. The left side of your brain deals with logical ordering and sequences, while the right side of your brain deals with imagination and creativity. We're going to come up with a logical ordering of locations that we're familiar with, and will then use our imagination to link vivid mental imagery to those locations. The imagery will represent the information we want to remember.

The first step is to make sure we know the locations in order. This will be very easy, because we're going to be using a very natural ordering of locations on our body, starting from the bottom and moving up to the top. The first location is your left foot. The second location is your right foot. The third location is your knees. The fourth location is your waist. The fifth location is your belly button. The sixth location is your chest. The seventh location is your neck. The eighth location is your mouth. The ninth location is your nose. And the tenth location is the top of your head. Again, that's: left foot, right foot, knees, waist, belly button, chest, neck, mouth, nose, top of head. As you learn these in order, I'd like you to either wiggle or point to each location on your body. Don't move on to the next paragraph until you are able to recite each location to yourself, in order, without any mistakes.

Go ahead and do it now.

Now that you know all the locations on your body in the order I specified, you can use those locations to store information! Yes, places on your body can actually act as mental filing cabinets! Let me show you how.

I'm going to have you memorize the following list of words in order:

apple
watch
umbrella
racket
car
football
bee

24

earring

stapler

comb.

Again, I'm going to have you exercise your imagination as I did earlier, but this time you're going to make use of the locations on your body. I'm going to really have you get a lot of your senses involved. Some of what I'm going to ask you to imagine might seem ludicrous, some might seem painful, some of it might even seem scary. But that's the point! If you really get your senses involved and experience the imagery, then you won't forget the information even if you try! Don't focus on having to remember anything, but rather just relax and have fun with this! OK, here we go.

Imagine that underneath your left foot is a large apple. You are rolling that apple around with your left foot. Really try to feel it under your foot. Now imagine that you begin to stomp on the apple and smash it up. You smash it up so much in fact that it begins to turn into applesauce. Try your best to experience this as if it were actually happening. On your right foot, you notice that there is a watch strapped to it. The watch begins ticking really loudly. It's ticking faster and faster, louder and louder. All of a sudden, the glass part of the watch shatters! You look at your knees and see a giant umbrella attached to them. You reach over and push the button to open the umbrella, and when you do, water splashes all over your face as the umbrella opens!

All of a sudden, you feel a pain in the side of your waist. It really hurts and feels like something is lodged in your side. You look and see a handle sticking out of your side. You pull on the handle and out slides a racket! Unbelievably, there was a racket lodged in your waist! Now, you feel and hear rumbling coming from near your belly button. The rumbling is getting louder and louder. It begins to actually sound like an engine. Suddenly, a car shoots out of your belly button! You can hear the car's engine roaring and can see its tyres spinning. *Bam!* Something has just hit you in the chest. You look and see that a football is continuously hitting you in the chest. You struggle to try and stop it, but you can't. The football just keeps hitting you in the chest and there is nothing that you can do about it. As if things couldn't get any worse, now you see and hear a bee. It's buzzing and circling your neck. You are afraid that it might sting, and then without warning it does start stinging you in the neck. Now, you feel a pain coming from your mouth. Your tongue is stinging and you feel something attached to it. You pull on the object and see that it's an earring! As you pull on the earring, it stretches your tongue.

As if enough things on your body weren't already hurting, you now feel pain coming from your nose. In addition, you can't breathe through it any longer. It must have something to do with this stapler that you see continuously stapling your nostrils together! You now feel a sudden urge to comb your hair and luckily there already seems to be a comb stuck in it. You begin using the comb, but it starts to pull out your hair! *Ouch!*

It should now be very easy for you to recall the list of random words in order, by merely thinking of each part of your body in the order outlined earlier. When you think of your left foot, the apple should come to mind. When you think of your right foot, the watch should come to mind. When you think of your knees, the umbrella should come to mind. When you think of your waist, the racket should come to mind. When you think of your belly button, the car should come to mind. When you think of your chest, the football should come to mind. When you think of your neck, the bee should come to mind. When you think of your mouth, the earring should come to mind. When you think of your nose, the stapler should come to mind. When you think of the top of your head, the comb should come to mind.

Close your eyes and try it. Amazing, isn't it?

This Body Method is a powerful and easy to learn memory improvement technique. It is also expandable. There are many other body parts that you could add to the list to make it longer in order to give you more filing cabinets. Your ears, eyes, eyebrows, and elbows are just a few possibilities. You can use whatever body parts you like as long as you learn them in a specific order before using them. Although this technique is extensible, it does have its limits. At some point, you might want to memorize a long list and will run out of body parts to use. Even with this limitation, however, it is a powerful tool to add to your memory toolbox.

The Peg List

With the two techniques that we've covered so far, if I were to ask you for the fifth word in a list, you would need to traverse the four previous words before being able to give me the fifth. I'm now going to teach you a technique that will allow you to instantly tell me the nth word or piece of information from a list. This technique is known as a Peg List. The easiest type of peg list to learn is a number/rhyme list. In this type of list, each element of the list rhymes with its corresponding number. Here is the list that we are going to use:

1-gun
2-shoe
3-tree
4-door
5-hive
6-bricks
7-heaven
8-plate
9-wine
10-hen.

I want you to now take a few minutes to learn this list in order. As you do, for each of the words in the list, I want you to see an image in your mind that corresponds to the word. For instance, for 1-gun, you should picture a gun and really try to see it clearly in your mind.

Now that you've taken a few minutes to learn the number/rhyme peg list and are able to recite it in order, I'm going to teach you how to apply it to learning a random list of words. This is going to be very similar to what we did with the body list, except that instead of linking vivid imagery to locations on our body, we will be linking vivid imagery to each of the elements on the peg list. The list of random words that we are going to learn is as follows:

remote
card
book
calculator
phone
box
candle
star
wax
watermelon.

As always, just relax and enjoy yourself as we go through the imagery. Here we go. I want you to imagine that you pick up a remote and start to use it as a gun. You can actually shoot bullets out of the remote and it makes a loud bang with each shot that you take! Next, imagine that you are walking around and feel something in your shoe. It's really bothering you, so you decide to take off your shoe and see what it is. You reach inside your shoe and pull out a card. How did that get in there?

You now look out of your window and see the strangest thing. It's a tree like none you've ever seen before. On the tip of the tree, you see a book. The book is gigantic and actually looks as if it is growing out of the tree. You can see the pages of the book turning as the wind blows. Next, you see a door magically appear in front of you. You can't help but feel curious and want to open the door. You try, but it's locked. On the door, you notice what isn't a keypad, but actually a calculator. You punch in a bunch of computations, and finally after hitting the = sign one last time, the door opens. Now, you'd like to make a phone call, but your phone is trapped inside a hive. Bees are buzzing around it and you are afraid to reach in and get it.

Finally, you muster up the courage, but sure enough you're stung as you grab your phone out of the hive. You now look outside your window and see yet another strange sight. Bricks are flying through the air and they keep smashing into a huge box. The bricks seem to be coming from nowhere and just keep hitting the box, until it is finally quite smashed. What was that about? You now think of heaven and see it clearly in your mind. It's beautiful. All of a sudden, you see a large candle being lowered down from heaven. The candle is burning brighter and brighter. Soon the flame from the candle becomes so bright that it hurts your eyes.

You are now feeling hungry so go into your cupboard for a plate. The plate you take out is not like any you've ever seen before. You have no idea where you got it. The plate has a star on it, and you can actually see the star twinkling. You examine the plate thoroughly and can't seem to find any logical explanation for how this star on the plate could be twinkling so brightly. Instead of getting something to eat, you now feel like having a drink. You open your favourite bottle of wine, but there is something terribly wrong. There is no wine inside. The bottle is filled with wax!

Really try to experience what that would feel like. You are looking forward to drinking some of your favourite wine, but find the bottle is filled with wax. I want you to now picture seeing a huge hen. The hen is clucking loudly and it's pecking at a watermelon. You didn't know that hens ate watermelons, but this hen seems to be thoroughly enjoying a watermelon. As it pecks the watermelon, you can see pieces of the melon splattering everywhere.

After seeing all those unusual images in your mind, it should now be very easy to recall the list of random words just by thinking of each element of the number/rhyme peg list. Also, if I ask you to give me the fifth word in the list, you should immediately think of hive (5 = hive), which will make you think of the phone. If asked for the seventh word, you should think of heaven (7 = heaven) and will thus be reminded of the candle.

Now put the book down and remember the whole list. Did you ever think that memorizing and remembering could be so fun and easy? Well, it's only going to get better from here!

The Journey Method

We're now going to learn my favourite memory improvement technique. It's the tool that I've used most often over the years while competing in memory competitions. The technique is very powerful and probably the most easily extensible of all of the techniques covered in this book. Once mastered, it will allow you to build up an endless supply of mental filing cabinets. This particular technique has a very long history and has been known by a number of different names. It seems to have originated with the ancient Greeks, and was known as the Method of Loci. It was later used by the Roman orators to memorize long speeches and texts, and became known as the Roman Room Method. Nowadays, it is used by modern memorizers like myself and is often referred to as the Journey Method.

Like the body list that we learned earlier, the Journey Method utilizes both sides of your brain to encode information, and involves linking vivid mental imagery to an ordered sequence of locations that you are familiar with. Instead of using locations on your body, however, you use locations from a familiar environment. For example, you could use locations from your home or apartment, grocery store, favourite shopping mall, friend's place, local gym, etc. Just as with the body list, the first step is to learn the locations in order and be able to mentally traverse them in sequence. In order to help you get a feel for what a journey is and the types of locations that a typical journey can contain, I'm going to walk you through one that I've used many times throughout the years in competitions. I often use my apartment and imagine walking through it and looking at the following locations in order:

front door
cupboard
refrigerator
stove
kitchen sink
microwave
television
coffee table
couch
easy chair
bedroom mirror
closet
bathroom sink

bathtub

toilet

bedroom lamp

window sill

head of the bed

foot of the bed

dresser.

You will notice that there are 20 different locations along my journey. Every time I use this particular "apartment journey", I mentally traverse the 20 locations in the same sequence every time. This allows me to memorize information in order, just as you were able to do with the body list, once you learned the locations on your body in a certain order. Once you know the order of the locations, you can then link vivid imagery to each location. Again, the vivid imagery will represent the information that you want to remember.

I'm going to teach you the Journey Method by having you go through a fun exercise that will not only give you a good handle on using the Journey Method, but will also illustrate just how powerful everything that you've learned so far really is. Shortly, you are going to be able to quickly and easily memorize and perfectly recall the top 20 countries in Europe ranked by Gross Domestic Product (GDP)!

The first step is to establish a journey. Using my example as a guide, I want you to choose

20 locations from your residence and learn them in order. The sequence of the locations should be natural. In other words, you should learn them in the order in which you would encounter them if you were going to take a certain route around your residence. Please make sure that you can mentally traverse through each location on your journey, in the same order, at least a few times before continuing to the next paragraph.

Go ahead. Start with the front door ...

Now that you've established a journey and are able to mentally traverse it in order, we are going to use it to memorize the following list of European countries in order by their GDP:

Germany
United Kingdom
France
Italy
Russia
Spain
Netherlands
Turkey
Switzerland
Sweden
Poland
Belgium
Norway

Austria
Denmark
Finland
Ireland
Greece
Portugal
Czech Republic.

At your first location, I want you to imagine that you see a giant German Shepherd! The dog is walking around and barking really loudly. The barking is so loud in fact that it starts to really startle you! Try to see and hear this happening at this location of your journey as best you can. The "German" Shepherd will be enough to remind you of "Germany".

At your next location, you see two gigantic castles. The castles are two different colours and are at first separate from each other. Visualize this to the best of your ability. Suddenly, an explosion occurs that causes the two castles to join together. Think of these two castles joined together as being the "United Kingdom". At the next location of your journey, you see the Eiffel Tower! This iconic landmark suddenly begins to spin, then it stops, only to begin spinning once more. The Eiffel Tower will of course remind you of "France".

You continue along your journey to the next location and notice that it is completely covered in pizza, ravioli, and spaghetti with meatballs. All of this

"Italian" food will help you to think of "Italy". Russia is famous for its vodka, so you see vodka bottle after vodka bottle continuously shooting out of the next location of your journey. This will help you to remember that "Russia" is next. At the next location, you see a bullfighting matador covering the spot with his red cape. The matador then lifts the cape up before once again covering up the location. This will help to remind you of "Spain", which is famous for its bullfighting.

You look at your journey's next location and see a man and woman there dancing in wooden shoes. You are fascinated by their shoes and the sounds that the shoes are making while they dance. These wooden shoes will help to remind you of the "Netherlands". At the next location of your journey, you see a delicious looking roasted turkey with stuffing and cranberry sauce accompanying it. You decide to go ahead and eat some of the turkey, which does indeed taste delicious. This will remind you of "Turkey".

A giant Rolex watch covers the next location. This Rolex is unlike any that you've ever seen before. The face of the watch dial is made of cheese, and the hands of the watch are made of chocolate! This will surely remind you of "Switzerland", which is known for wonderful watches, cheese, and chocolate.

There is a giant bowl of Swedish meatballs at your next location. You try to eat the meatballs, but every time you reach for one, it magically jumps out of your reach. Eventually, you manage to take a bite of one of the meatballs and it immediately makes you think of "Sweden".

At the following location of your journey, you find a large brass pole similar to those you would find in a fire station. You climb up the pole and then slide down the pole, which you find to be a really fun experience. This "pole" will be enough to remind you of "Poland". The next location is completely covered in Belgian waffles. The syrup on the waffles is very sticky, almost like glue, so it's very difficult for you to pry off one of the waffles, but you are eventually able to. These waffles will remind you of "Belgium".

A Viking is hitting the next location of your journey with a giant hammer. Vikings are a famous part of the history of "Norway". At the next location, you are surprised to see Arnold Schwarzenegger lifting weights and reciting his famous line "I'll be back!" This will remind you of Schwarzenegger's home country of "Austria". The next location of your journey somehow contains the entrance to a large den. You enter the den and find that the walls are covered in large dark marks. A den with marks is going to remind you of "Denmark".

You discover that the next location of your journey is completely covered in shark fins! This will easily remind you of "Finland". At the next location of your journey, you see a rainbow! Suddenly, a leprechaun slides down the rainbow with a pot of gold! This leprechaun will get you to think of "Ireland". Lightning bolts are zapping the next location of your journey and you notice that they are being thrown by Zeus! This will serve to remind you of "Greece".

Cristiano Ronaldo is playing football at the next location of your journey. Ronaldo is a famous footballer from "Portugal". The last location of your journey is covered with pints of Pilsner beer. You drink some of the beer and think to yourself that some of the best beer in the world comes from the "Czech Republic".

At this point, I'd like you to take a mental stroll back through all of the locations of your journey and review all of the imagery at each location. You should now be able to name all of the top 20 European countries in order by GDP! It should be apparent at this point just how powerful and useful the Journey Method can be.

You now have a solid foundation in the fundamentals of memory improvement. The techniques you've learned in this chapter will allow you to dramatically improve your ability to remember important information. And, as with anything else in life, the more you practise, the better you will get and the more improvement you will see. If you continue your training, you will soon develop powerful memory skills that will benefit you for the rest of your career. In addition, as you can no doubt tell from going through the exercises, practising these techniques is also wonderful exercise for your brain!

3
Build Better Business Relationships

One of the most important business skills you can develop is the ability to remember the names of people you meet. It is an age-old truth that people love hearing the sound of their own name. If you think about it for a second you'll realize that you already instinctively know this to be true. The most popular people at work, at school, at sports and social clubs, and other organizations you may be involved with, tend to know everyone's name. And it's a fact of life that remembering people's names helps to build better business and personal relationships.

There is no avoiding that learning someone's name and calling them by it is an integral part of getting to know someone that really helps to build rapport with the person. The opposite is also true! If you are not remembering people's names, or perhaps, even worse, are calling people by the wrong name, this can be detrimental to both business and personal relationships. As I briefly discussed in the opening chapter, the importance of remembering names has implications for career advancement, business networking, customer service, and much more.

So, how do you develop this skill that can be so essential to business success? Let's first address the most common reason why we tend to forget the names of people we meet – we just aren't paying enough attention to begin with! It may seem obvious, but many times when someone introduces themselves to us, we just don't really pay any attention to their name. Our mind is wandering elsewhere to things such as: their looks, their profession or position, our own nerves, our surroundings, what we're going to eat for dinner later, etc. Often our minds are focused on just about anything and everything other than the person's name! Even myself, a national memory champion who can open presentations by naming hundreds of people in the audience after hearing each name only one time, will not remember someone's name if when they are telling me their name, my mind is on a double fault that I hit in my tennis match earlier, or what they'll be serving for dinner later at the conference. There is no getting around the fact that in order to remember someone's name, you must *focus* on it for at least one to two seconds. The following four simple steps will help you to do this:

Step #1

Immediately repeat the name and shake the person's hand. If you are introduced to someone named

John, you will say something to the effect of "Nice to meet you, John", or "Pleased to meet you, John", while shaking his hand. Or you might even say the name first: "John, so nice to meet you". This forces you to focus and pay attention to the name. That's the only way you would be able to repeat the person's name back to them while shaking their hand.

Step #2

Early on in your interaction with the person, use their name while asking them any simple question. "So John, how do you know Chester?" or "John, what brings you to the meeting today?" are examples of doing this. I want to emphasize here that I am only recommending that you ask *one* simple question using the person's name early on in your interaction. It is not necessary and in fact I do *not* recommend that you use the person's name repeatedly during your conversation. One question using the name will suffice to help keep the name in your mind and prevent it from just going in one ear and out the other.

Step #3

Think of a connection between the person's name and anything at all that you already know. I really do mean *anything.* The name John might make you think of John Lennon, the Gospel of John in the Bible, John F. Kennedy, or it could even simply be that you have a friend or family member that is also named John. Thinking of a connection between the name and literally anything that you already know will really help the name to stick well in your mind.

Step #4

Say goodbye to the person using their name. Before you leave the party, meeting, wedding, or whatever other type of function you may be at, make sure to say goodbye to the people that you've met using their names. A simple "Goodbye, John" or "Until next time, John" or "Nice talking with you, John" will go a long way toward cementing the name in your mind and give you a much better chance of remembering it the next time you see the person.

The four steps I've outlined above should be fairly easy for you to put into practice right away. They will help you to put more focus on people's names when you are meeting them. In addition, being sure to implement these steps as much as possible, will help you to take control of the social interaction when being introduced to people. If someone is trying to introduce you to a group of people in rapid succession: John, Nancy, Oscar, Liz, Tim, and so on, remembering the names can become very difficult even for someone at my skill level.

So, I recommend that you try to take control and slow the process down by at least implementing the first step above. If this isn't possible given the situation that you find yourself in, you could even implement the steps immediately following the rapid fire introductions. Given the case of introductions in rapid succession, it's perfectly acceptable to ask for a person's name again or verify it while starting with the first step: "You were John, correct?" or "I'm sorry, I *missed* your name given the rapid introductions, you were...?" Then, continue with the remaining steps as you can.

In addition to not paying enough attention to begin with, another reason why we have difficulty remembering names is that names are abstract and we don't readily *see* them in our minds. It's very common for people to say "I never forget a *face!*" However, it is not common for people to say "I never forget a *name!*" Just about everyone at some point in their life has experienced the situation in which upon seeing someone you may have met even many years ago, you immediately remember the fact that you've met them before. You can remember the person's face, but you can't seem to remember the name. This is commonplace.

Let me describe another scenario that happens to us often. Let's say you go to a party with one of your friends and you both meet a lot of new people at this party. Two weeks after the party, you're talking with your friend who accompanied you to the party and your friend describes someone to you that you both met at the party. Your friend says something like, "Remember the gentleman that we met at the party who's an attorney? The one that said he's a member of the tennis club?" Given just that little bit of a description of the guy from the party, often both you and your friend are very quickly and easily able to pull up in your mind an image of the guy from the party. It's easy for you both to remember what the guy looks like, but neither one of you can manage to remember his name. This is also a commonplace experience. (And imagine how impressed your friend will be if you say, "Oh yeah, Jack Olsen".)

Why do the two scenarios that I just described happen to us so often? It's because when we meet people, we actually *see* their face with our eyes and the face is recorded into our visual memory, which is very powerful, but we never actually *see* the person's name. In order to become better at remembering names, we must learn to turn the name into a powerful and memorable *image* that we are able to clearly *see* in our minds. Once you've turned a person's name into an image that you can picture, you need only connect or link that image visually to the person in some way. That may sound a bit complex at first, but there are many ways to go about it and it's actually all very easy as you'll soon realize!

In the previous chapter, you learned to link images that remind you of what you want to remember to locations on your body. You can do something similar to help you remember a person's name, but in this case the images will go on the other person's body instead of your own. When you meet someone, ask yourself how this particular person looks *unique* to you. This unique thing about the person's look could be a particular facial feature or something about the person's look overall. Once you've decided on the unique aspect to the person, you'll want to exaggerate it in your mind in some way. This exaggerated unique aspect to the person will now serve as the storage place for the person's name.

Next, think of an image that will in some way, *any* way, remind you of the name. The image might remind you of the name based on sound. For instance, a *chain* might remind you of the name *Jane*. Alternatively, your images might be more symbolic. For example, a *white rabbit* to remind you of *Alice*, or perhaps a dumbbell (gym) to remind you of Jim. (But be really careful not to say "So nice to meet you, dumbbell"!)

There are various ways in which an image might remind you of a particular name. Once you've decided on your image for the name, you'll simply use your imagination to vividly link the image to the unique aspect of the person.

While linking the image to the person, it's important to keep in mind the principles that you learned in Chapter 2. Try to vividly see the imagery as best you can, involve additional senses as you can, and also be sure to try to make this all crazy, unusual, and extraordinary in some way.

Let's jump into an example illustrating using imagery along with a unique aspect of a person's look to memorize the person's name. If you meet a guy named Jim who in your opinion has large ears, you might imagine his ears as being gigantic and see them swinging from the side of his head. Next, you might visualize a dumbbell twirling around in each of his ears! A *dumbbell* would remind you of going to the *gym* and thus the name *Jim*. If you vividly experience what I just described happening in your mind, the next time you see Jim, you'll once again notice his ears as you did before and all of the vivid imagery will immediately come back to your mind causing you to remember his name.

What if you meet a woman named Jane that you think has very beautiful hair? You might visualize her hair growing out longer and longer. As it's doing this, a pleasant aroma starts to emit from her hair. Then, a sparkling chain appears and begins to weave itself throughout her hair. *Chain* should be enough to remind you of *Jane*. Take just five seconds or less to vividly experience this happening, and I promise you that the next time you see Jane you will immediately remember her name!

Note that the image that reminds you of the person's name could actually be a person with the same name, instead of an object. So instead of seeing a chain, you might imagine *Jane Eyre* getting tangled up in the hair.

An alternate way to go about committing someone's name to memory is to use your imagination to take the unique aspect about them that you've exaggerated in your mind and mentally place that aspect on someone you already know with the same name. Let me illustrate how this would work with the Jim and Jane just discussed above.

Instead of putting a dumbbell in each of Jim's giant ears that are swinging from the side of his head, you can simply visualize a friend of yours named Jim having these giant ears swinging from the side of his head. If you vividly experience the sight of your *friend Jim* with those giant swinging ears, the next time you see the *new Jim* that you've just met, upon noticing his ears once again, you'll immediately remember that you placed those ears on your *friend Jim*, thus this new person's name is also *Jim*. With Jane, we imagined that her hair was growing out longer and longer, and a pleasant aroma started to emit from her hair. Simply imagine this happening to a friend of yours named Jane. Then, when you later see the new Jane that you just met, you should once again notice her hair as you did before. The imagery of the hair growing out with the pleasant aroma will return to your mind.

Next, just ask yourself where you placed that special hair. You'll remember that you visualized it on your *friend Jane*, thus this new woman's name is also *Jane!*

You can also commit a person's name to memory by focusing in on how this person in some way looks like someone that you already know that shares the same name. The person you already know doesn't need to be someone that you necessarily know *personally*. It could be a famous person or even a character from one of your favourite TV shows or movies. Upon meeting a person named Matt and asking yourself how he looks unique to you, you might notice that he has a nose that looks a lot like Matt Damon's nose. Focusing in on that physical similarity between the two Matts might be enough to lock this new Matt's name into your mind, and it's fine to stop there.

However, I'd recommend taking it even one step further and after focusing in on the similar-looking noses, I'd visualize Matt Damon morphing into a new version of himself so that he turns into this new guy that you've just met named Matt. If you vividly experience this happening in your mind, upon once again seeing the Matt that you've recently met, you'll immediately notice his nose as you did before. This will trigger the memory of *Matt Damon* morphing into this new guy and you'll know that this guy's name is also *Matt*.

With the Matt example, we focused on a *particular* facial feature, but keep in mind that you can instead focus on an aspect of the person's look *overall*. If you meet someone named *Dwayne* that is extremely muscular like *Dwayne "The Rock" Johnson*, you might imagine "The Rock" morphing into another version of himself, which is this new person that you are meeting also named *Dwayne*.

Let me quickly summarize the three basic visual-based techniques for remembering names that I've covered in this chapter:

1. Exaggerate something unique about the person and place an image there that will remind you of the person's name.

2. Exaggerate something unique about the person and mentally place that exaggerated aspect on someone you already know with the same name.

3. Focus in on a physical similarity between the person you're meeting and someone you already know while visualizing one person morphing into the other.

The techniques I've described will take some practice but after using them for a month or less, you are definitely going to dramatically improve your ability to remember the names of people you meet. When first starting out with the visual-based techniques for names, you may find that it takes you longer than you'd like to come up with images to remind you of certain names. This is perfectly normal. With practice, you will become faster and faster at coming up with your images. It is also useful to have some particular images for certain names preset and ready for immediate use should you happen to meet people with those names. For this reason, I've provided you with some names and corresponding images that you might like to use below:

James = River Thames, James Spader, jam(s)

John = toilet bowl, John Lennon

Robert = row boat, row of Berts, Robert Redford

Michael = archangel, L-shaped mic, Michael Jackson

William = wheel with yam(s), Will.I.Am, William Shakespeare

David = Statue of David, diving video, David Bowie

Richard = rich orchard, rice chard, Richard Branson

Charles = charred Ls, Prince Charles

Joseph = joe (coffee) siphon, Joseph Gordon-Levitt

Thomas = English muffin, toe mess, Thomas Edison

Christopher = Christ with fur, cross-shaped topper, Christopher Columbus

Daniel = doe kneel(ing), Daniel Radcliffe

Paul = pill, "P" on a wall, McCartney

Mark = marker, a scuff mark, Mark Twain

Donald = dough nailed, Donald Trump, Donald Duck

George = gorge, George Bush

Kenneth = can in a net, Kenneth Branagh

Steven = stove-in, stove with "N" coming out, Steven Spielberg

Edward = Edward Scissorhands, IT wired, Edward Norton

Brian = brain, bran, Brian Cranston

Mary = a wedding, Mary Poppins, Virgin Mary, the Queen Mary

Patricia = pat on the back, putting rice, Patricia Arquette

Linda = lint, leaning "D", Linda Ronstadt, Linda Hamilton

Barbara = barbed wire, barbed bear, Barbara Walters, Barbara Streisand

Elizabeth = casino chip with "Z" on it for a bet, Elizabeth Taylor

Jennifer = gin bottle with fur on it, Jennifer Garner, Jennifer Aniston

Maria = marrying apples, scene from West Side Story, Maria Sharapova

Susan = getting sued, sue sand, sun with sand, Susan Sarandon

Margaret = a margarita, margarine, Margaret Thatcher

Dorothy = yellow brick road, Doritos on a tree, Dorothy Hamill

Lisa = lease with an "A", lice in shape of "A", Lisa Simpson, Mona Lisa

Nancy = nuns in the sea, naan in the sea, Nancy Reagan, Nancy Pelosi

Karen = scene depicting caring, carrying something, corn, Karen Allen

Betty = casino chips to place bet, bat tea, Betty Boop, Betty Crocker

Helen = 1000 ships, hailing cab, Helen Mirren

Sandra = sand with a drier, sand draw, Sandra Bullock

Donna = the dawn with an "A" rising, doughnut, Donna Karan

Carol = Christmas carol, people caroling, Carol Burnett

Ruth = Babe Ruth, root, Book of Ruth, Dr Ruth

Sharon = people sharing, Cher on something, Sharon Osbourne, Sharon Stone

The ability to remember the names of clients, customers, and anyone else you meet, is priceless. I hope you'll begin this very day to put into practice everything you've learned in this chapter. If so, you will soon develop an invaluable skill that will benefit you for the rest of your life!

4

Impress in the Boardroom

At some point during your career you'll likely be required to give some sort of speech or presentation. Your audience could be a small group of superiors in the boardroom or an entire auditorium of peers.

Your presentations will be much more well-received and impressive if you can minimize the amount of notes you use or, even better, eliminate notes altogether. Many trial attorneys have been through my memory training programmes. They've informed me that if they lose eye contact with the jury during opening and closing arguments in order to look through their notes, they lose the jury's attention and are much less persuasive than an attorney that can smoothly cover all the key points of their case from memory, i.e. without notes.

Speakers at conferences who do nothing but read one slide after another tend to bore their audiences and don't usually receive the best evaluations. You will always be much more impressive and persuasive with your speeches and presentations if you are able to skillfully give them mostly, if not entirely, from memory without referring to notes or cue cards.

So how do you go about developing this valuable business skill? I recommend going about it in the same way as one of the most famous public speakers of all time. Cicero (Marcus Tullius Cicero) from ancient Rome was an orator renowned for his public speaking skills. He was able to give lengthy speeches eloquently from memory alone, orations that were very effective and persuasive. His secret? You already learned it in Chapter 2!

Cicero stored images that reminded him of the key points of his speeches along a familiar path or *journey*. You learned the Journey Method in Chapter 2 and applied it to memorizing the top 20 countries in Europe by their GDP. Applying the Journey Method in a similar manner will help you to easily memorize speeches and presentations. In this chapter, I will guide you through this simple process.

The first step is to research your topic and, based on that research, create an outline of all the main points and subpoints that you'd like to get across to your audience. Next, count to see how many total points you ended up with. After this, come up with a *journey* that has a number of locations equal to the number of points of your speech. If you have 12 points that you need to get across to your audience, then your journey must consist of 12 locations. Next, you'll need to utilize all the principles that you learned in Chapter 2 in order to come up with imagery that will remind you in some way of the points and then subsequently link that imagery to the corresponding locations of your journey. Imagery that will remind you of the first point will go at the first location of your journey, imagery that will remind you of the second point will go at the second location of your journey, and so on.

When implementing this last step, remember to employ the main memory improvement principles of visualization, additional senses, and also using your creativity and imagination to make sure that what you are seeing and experiencing in your mind is crazy, unusual, and extraordinary. Once you've completed this four-step process, you can easily recall your entire presentation by simply taking a mental stroll back through your journey. The images that you've placed at the various locations should effectively remind you of the points that you need to communicate to your audience.

Let's now move forward with a sample presentation to further clarify the process. Below is an outline for a short talk about autonomous (self-driving) cars based on a little research that I did.

Is switching to autonomous cars best for our future?

Many people say "Yes" for the following reasons:

    a. Autonomous cars will save your life; most accidents are caused by human error.

b. Autonomous cars will save you time; you can work, read, or sleep while the self-driving car takes you to your destination.

c. Autonomous cars will save you money; with fewer accidents happening, insurance prices are likely to drop dramatically.

However, many people say "No" to autonomous cars for the following reasons:

a. Autonomous cars could kill you; a computer program error or hacker attack could cause this.

b. Autonomous cars could take your job; taxis and delivery drivers wouldn't be needed anymore.

c. Autonomous cars could hinder your privacy; every trip that you make will likely be logged and tracked somewhere.

So, is switching to autonomous cars best for our future?

I'd say "Yes", but only if the technology can be developed well enough to protect against computer errors, hackers, and loss of privacy.

The first step that I listed was to create an outline based on your research. That's just been provided above. Next, was to count up all of the total points. In this case, there are 11 in total including the Roman numerals and lower case letters. We now want to come up with an 11-location *journey*. Go ahead and decide on 11 locations. You may want to use your current residence, office, grocery store, pharmacy, athletic club, train station, or mall. Review the locations mentally until you are able to recite all 11 of them easily from memory by simply taking a mental stroll through the locations in order. Now that you have your journey ready to go, you can proceed with using it to commit the presentation to memory. Let's do that together now.

At the first location of your journey, I'd like you to visualize a car driving around without a driver. The landscape that you see the car driving around looks very futuristic. You may even want to imagine hearing some sort of futuristic sounds. (Maybe the original scores from "Star Trek" or "Star Wars".) Remember, the more senses that you involve and the more crazy and unusual you make what you are experiencing in your mind, the more memorable it's all going to be.

This scenario happening at the first location of your journey will remind you to state the title of your presentation, something to the effect of "Are Autonomous Cars Best for Our Future?" Note that this does not *exactly* match what's in the outline. What you are doing by attaching imagery to the various locations of your journey is creating mental "cue cards" to simply remind you of the point that you are trying to get across to your audience, and it is most effective to do this with different wording each time as long as you are effectively communicating the point that you are trying to make.

At the next location of your journey, visualize a crowd of demonstrators walking around and waving giant signs that say "Yes". That should be enough to remind you to say something close to "Many people say 'Yes' for the following reasons". Even if that imagery reminded you to say only "Many people say 'Yes'", that would be effective enough to get the point across. When committing a speech or presentation to memory, it's very important not to get caught up in trying to memorize the entire thing or even your outline word for word. This is because even if you do recite it perfectly word for word from memory, it will come off as very monotonous and sound to your audience almost as if you are reading it from a sheet of paper. It's important to realize that you only need mental cues to remind you of the points on your outline and that you then just need to effectively communicate the points to your audience.

At the third location of your journey, I'd like you to picture two cars with drivers about to crash into each at full speed, but then an autonomous car with arms coming out of its doors and a cape attached to the bumper flies in "Superman-like" from above to swoop down and carry off one of the cars to safety. This funny scenario should help you to say something similar to "Autonomous cars will save your life from accidents caused by human driving errors".

At your journey's next location, I'd like you to visualize an unusually large clock. The clock opens up and a construction worker walks out reading a purple book before he starts to fall asleep. This could help you to say something to the effect of "They will save time for you to work, read, and sleep".

Your next location has an autonomous car driving around with money and insurance documents flying continuously out of the windows. This should remind you to next let your audience know that "Autonomous cars will save you money on insurance".

At the next location of your journey, I'd like you to picture another bunch of demonstrators waving around giant signs that have pictures of autonomous cars with large "X's" going through them. This will prompt you to next say something like "However, some people say 'No' to the idea of autonomous cars".

At your journey's next location, you see a giant computer with the message "ERROR" flashing continuously across its screen before it violently explodes. This will remind you to let your audience know that people are concerned that "Autonomous cars could kill you due to computer error".

Visualize a gigantic briefcase at the next location of your journey. A taxi and delivery truck both drive by the briefcase and it suddenly explodes causing the taxi and truck to explode as well. This imagery will remind you to tell your audience that "Jobs could be lost, including those of taxis and delivery trucks".

At the next location of your journey, you see an autonomous car that has hundreds of eyes built into its exterior. The eyes seem to be watching you as it drives over first a series of logs and then a series of tracks. This will cue you to explain to your audience that "Autonomous cars might affect your privacy due to logging and tracking".

The next location of your journey has many autonomous cars driving around a futuristic look-ing landscape with a giant question mark visi-ble in the background. This will get you to ask your audience: "Given the points just presented, are autonomous cars good for our future?"

The last location of your journey has a pile of elec-tronic gadgets that start to move around and stick together to form a large shield. This shield then starts to cover a computer with error messages on its screen, a group of people that look like computer hackers, and also a pile of eyeballs that look as if they're watching you. Thinking of this image will allow you to conclude your presentation with "I'd say 'Yes' if the technology can be developed to pro-tect against computer errors, hackers, and privacy issues."

You should now be able to give the autonomous car presentation from memory, hitting on every point and subpoint in order by simply taking a mental

stroll through the locations of your journey and seeing the imagery that you've placed at each location.
If you're having difficulty remembering any of the
points, you just need to adjust the imagery at the
corresponding location of your journey. Of course,
the more you review your journey and the images
at its various locations, the more smoothly you'll be
able to give your presentation from memory without notes.

You've just started to develop an incredibly valuable business skill. You may be an executive who
needs to give a presentation in front of the board; a
salesman addressing a target group; an entrepreneur
who needs to present your business idea to potential investors; a consultant giving a presentation to
potential clients; or maybe a professional who gives
presentations to peer groups.

Just continue to practise what you've learned in this
short chapter and you'll soon be impressing and per-
suading – just like Cicero!

5
Dealing with Numbers

B usiness professionals are frequently faced with the need to remember numerical information: phone numbers, dates, addresses, passwords, prices, formulas, figures, and more. People who can instantly and perfectly recall numbers that are stored in their mind come off as very impressive to colleagues in the boardroom, clients, and others as well. Remembering numbers more easily can help you a great deal in your career and in your personal life.

This chapter will teach you the most powerful and effective system for memorizing numbers that has ever been created. The system was developed more than 300 years ago by Stanislaus Mink von Wennsshein and is commonly referred to as the Phonetic Alphabet System, the "Major" System, and the Phonetic Mnemonic System. In this book, I will refer to it as the Phonetic Alphabet System.

In this system, each number between 0 and 9 has one or more phonetic consonant sounds associated with it. This is illustrated in the chart below:

Numbers	Sounds	Hints/Associations
0	s, z	Zero
1	t, d	1 downstroke (ta da)
2	n	2 downstrokes
3	m	3 downstrokes
4	r	Four
5	L	High five
6	ch, sh, j	6 & j both have hook shape
7	k, g	K Kellogg's
8	f, v	eight in middle
9	p, b	9 looks like an upside down b or p

The left hand column shows the numbers 0–9, the middle column shows the corresponding sounds, and the third column provides some hints and associations to help you commit the information from the first two columns to memory. Don't worry if this seems confusing at first. That's perfectly normal. Everything will begin to make sense shortly.

Before I have you start to commit the chart to memory, I'd like first to get you started with a working knowledge of how the system works. The Phonetic Alphabet System helps you take any number sequence and easily turn it into a word. Once you have a word for a number sequence, you can then produce in your mind a corresponding image. And once you have an image for a number sequence, you can then apply all of the powerful memory

techniques that you learned in previous chapters of this book that rely upon you turning the information that you're trying to remember into a series of memorable images.

As previously stated, the chart contains "consonant sounds". The consonant "letters" that you see in the chart are there to help you to learn the "sounds". For the number "0", the sounds associated with it are the phonetic sounds that the letters "s" and "z" make. You should be familiar with the sounds for those letters since most of us are taught to read phonetically.

For the number "1", the sounds associated with it are the phonetic sounds that the letters "t" and "d" make. For the number "2", the sound associated with it is the sound that the letter "n" makes. For the number "3", the sound associated with it is the sound that the letter "m" makes. For the number "4", the sound associated with it is the sound that the letter "r" makes. For the number "5", the sound associated with it is the sound that the letter "l" makes. For the number "6", the sounds associated with it are the phonetic sounds for the letter combinations "ch" and "sh", and also for the letter "j". For the number "7", the sounds associated with it are the phonetic sounds that the letters "k" and "g" make. For the number "8", the sounds associated with it are the phonetic sounds that the letters "f" and "v" make. For the number "9", the sounds associated with it are the phonetic sounds that the letters "p" and "b" make.

"Vowel sounds" can be used anywhere to help you to form words. Let's go over some examples. The number sequence "41" could correspond to the word "rat". In this case, we are using the "r" sound for the number "4", inserting the vowel sound "a", and then using the "t" sound for the number "1". Another possible word for the number sequence 41 could be the word "rod". In this case, we are using the "r" sound for the number "4", inserting the vowel sound "o", and then using the "d" sound for the number "1". Please note that 41 could also correspond to a longer word such as "read". The extra vowel sounds of "ea" in between the "r" and "d" sounds are perfectly acceptable with this system.

However, I'd like to point out that when choosing words for number sequences it is definitely preferable to use "nouns" whenever possible. This is because it is much easier to picture nouns and turn them into images, and there is also less ambiguity as to exactly what the image is that you are picturing when you are visualizing a simple noun as opposed to something more abstract. So, it would be preferable to use "rat" or "rod" for the number 41 instead of "read", even though using "read" would technically be in line with the rules of this particular form of the Phonetic Alphabet System.

For the number sequence "71" a possible word could be "kit", and another could be "kite". I'd like to point out that another possibility for "71" could be the word "cat". Although you don't see the letter "c" anywhere in the chart, the hard c "sound" is in fact the same as for the "k". Remember that this system is all about the sounds. The letters are really only in the chart in order to help you to learn the sounds. For this reason, the word "rice" could be used to represent the number "40". The consonant sounds in the word rice are "r" and "s", which correspond to "40". Below I'm going to give you some further examples. Please review them while referring to the chart as needed to make sure that you understand each one:

97 = book
07 = sock
49 = rope
30 = mouse
17 = dog
25 = nail
40 = rose
52 = lion
65 = shell
75 = coal
84 = fire
912 = button
126 = danish
750 = glass
641 = shirt

If the examples above make sense to you, then you already have a pretty good idea of how the phonetic alphabet system is supposed to work. Now, you just need to memorize the chart! That's the purpose of the third column of the chart with the hints and associations, which I'll now go over and clarify.

You see the word "zero" written in the third column of the first row in the chart? "Zero" begins with the "z" sound and also ends with an "o", which might remind you of a "0". This should help you to remember that the number "0" corresponds to the "z" sound. If you can remember "z" sound for "0", it should be should be fairly easy to remember the "s" sound for "0", because that is the only sound in the chart that sounds very similar to the "z" sound. I'd like you to now vocalize the "z" sound and note the position of your mouth and tongue. Next, vocalize the "s" sound and you'll note that your mouth and tongue position will be exactly the same as when you produce the "z" sound. This consistency of mouth and tongue position applies for all sounds that are on the same line as each other in the chart.

Let's continue with the third column of the second row in the chart. On a scrap sheet of paper, write down a "t" and note how many times your pen/pencil makes a downstroke. Do the same for the letter "d". When writing a "t" or "d", you will only make one downstroke. Keeping this in mind will help you to remember that for the number "1" (a downstroke when written), the corresponding sounds are "t" and "d". It may also be useful to think of the expression "ta da!" in order to help you to remember that the "t" and "d" sounds go together.

Looking at the third column of the third row in the chart will show you that you can remember that the "n" sound corresponds to the number "2" by thinking of the fact that when you write the letter "n" you will make exactly two downstrokes with your pen or pencil. Looking at the third column of the fourth row in the chart will show you that you can remember that the "m" sound corresponds to the number "3" by thinking of the fact that when you write the letter "m" you will make exactly three downstrokes with your pen or pencil.

Say the word "four" out loud and exaggerate the last sound of the word, which is the "r" sound. This will help you to understand the third column of the fifth row in the chart, which should remind you that the "r" sound corresponds to the number "4".

In the next row of the chart, the third column depicts a person's hand in the "high-five" position. With a hand in this position, you'll note the "L" shape that is formed by the index finger and thumb. Thinking about this should help you to remember that the "l" sound is associated with the number "5".

The next row of the chart shows the number "6" and the letter "J" side by side in the last column. Write down the number "6" and you'll note that it has a sort of hook shape to it just as is the case for the letter "J". This will help you to remember that the "J" sound is associated with the number "6", and if you can remember this it should be fairly easy to remember the similar sounds of "ch" and "sh".

In the next row of the chart, you'll find the letter "K" written similarly to how it appears on a Kellogg's cereal box. If you examine this particular "K" you'll notice a "7" on its left side and also a "7" on its right side that is oriented differently. Two "7" with the correct orientations can in fact be joined together in order to form an uppercase "K". This should help you to remember that the "K" sound is associated with the number "7". If you understand this, then it should be easy to remember the similar sound of "g". Thinking of the word "Kellogg's" might be useful to remind you that the "k" and g" sounds go together in the chart since "Kellogg's" has both the "k" and "g" sounds in it.

The next row of the chart depicts a lowercase cursive or scripted "f" in the last column. If you examine this particular "f" you'll notice two loops in the middle that look a bit like the number "8". This will help you to remember that the "f" sound is associated with the number "8". The "v" sound is the sound in the chart that is most similar to the "f" sound and should be easy to remember if you can remember the "f" sound. (Notice that your lips and teeth are in the same position when pronouncing either letter.)

The last row of the chart shows a "9", "p", and "b" in the last column. If you flip the number "9" around, it looks very much like a "p". If you then flip the "p" up it will look very much like a "b". So, different orientations of the number "9" can look like both the letters "p" and "b". Thinking of this should help you to remember that the "p" and "b" sounds are both associated with the number "9". It may also be useful to think of "peanut butter" in order to remind you that the "p" and "b" sounds go together in the chart.

I recommend that you review the chart and my explanations of the hints and associations for at least 10 minutes before you continue with the practical applications below. Try to commit the chart to memory.

Now that you know the Phonetic Alphabet System, you can begin to apply it in helping you to memorize any type of fact that has a number or figure associated with it. Let's go over the following examples:

- Doctor's phone number is 715-942-9142
- Dow Jones is up 95 points
- Stock price of Apple is 107.25
- The temperature in Paris is 17 degrees
- World War II ended in 1945.

You will always want to decide on a simple image to represent the fact part of the information, and then you will use the Phonetic Alphabet System to come up with an image or series of images for the number or figure part of the information. Once you have your images, you will use your creativity and imagination to visualize the images interacting together in an interesting and memorable way. You'll want to be sure to employ all of the principles that you learned in the earlier chapter entitled "The Building Blocks".

For the "doctor's phone number" above, you might decide on a simple image of a "stethoscope" to remind you of the fact part of the information. For the number or figure part of the information, you might visualize some "cattle" (k+t+l = 715) running into a "barn" (b+r+n = 942). These cattle then jump onto a "bed" (b+d = 91) before it starts to "rain" (r+n = 42) on them. Refer to the chart and study how I devised those words.

To link the fact to the figure, you could simply imagine the stethoscope first wrapping itself around the cattle, before the cattle run into the barn only to jump on a bed and get covered in rain. If you imagine all of that happening, then when you later need to recall the doctor's phone number, you'll easily remember the image sequence of "stethoscope", "cattle", "barn", "bed", "rain", and thus the number 715-942-9142.

For the fact about the "Dow Jones" above, you might decide on a simple image of an "electronic board with stock prices" to remind you of the fact part of the information. For the number or figure part of the information, you might visualize a giant "bell" (95). To then link the fact to the figure, you could simply imagine the electronic board getting smashed up by a giant bell. If you visualize that happening, then when you later need to recall how many points the Dow Jones is up, you'll easily remember the image sequence of "electronic board", "bell", and thus the number 95.

At this point you should be getting an idea of how the process works, so I'll shorten my explanations for the last three examples.

To commit to memory that the stock price of Apple Inc. is 107.25 you might visualize an "apple" (Apple Inc.) landing on a "disk" (107) that has a giant "nail" (25) going through it. Don't worry about the decimal point, because your mind will naturally recall where it belongs without the need for any imagery.

To remember that the temperature in Paris is 17 degrees, you might visualize the "Eiffel Tower" (Paris) with a "dog" (17) climbing up it.

To commit to memory the fact that World War II ended in 1945, you might visualize "Adolf Hitler" (World War II) getting crushed by a gigantic "roll" (45). For historical dates, it's usually sufficient to only commit the last two digits to memory, because by simply using your common sense and the context of the information you can usually determine the correct century. If the last two digits are not sufficient, then the last three digits should be.

Get some practice in now by using what you've just learned to commit to memory the following facts that contain figures (or you can create your own "facts" according to your specific geographic locale):

- Dentist's phone number is 972-941-7294
- Barack Obama is 54 years old
- Stock price of Facebook is 105.25
- The temperature in London 14 degrees
- The Korean War began in 1950.

Besides the fact that it is incredibly useful and impressive to be able to remember facts that contain figures, doing so is also wonderful exercise for your brain! If you would like a really effective brain workout, try memorizing long number sequences. Take the following 20-digit sequence and try to commit it to memory using the Story Method with 10 images, or by using the Journey Method with 10 images along a 10-location journey: 13492227468279749230.

You are no doubt already starting to realize the power of using the Phonetic Alphabet System to help you remember information that contains numbers. I encourage you to engage in practice with this system on a daily basis. Whenever you encounter a number anywhere in your environment, ask yourself if you can form a word from it. If the clock reads 1:27, you might think of a "tank". If you watch reads 1:21, you might think of a "tent". Take some time daily to look at the objects around you and ask yourself what number sequence those items correspond to. If you see a "table", sound it out and you should determine that it corresponds to the number sequence "195". If you see a door, you should think about it and realize that it corresponds to the number sequence "14". Trust me, diligent practising in this way as often as you can will have you fluent in the Phonetic Alphabet very quickly.

In order to gain tremendous speed in memorizing numbers, I highly recommend that you decide on preset images for every possible number sequence between 00 and 99. There are only 100 different combinations, so if you work on 10 a day for 10 days then you'll be done and will know your images for each number sequence pretty well. To help you, I've provided a list of possible words for you here:

00 Sauce	14 Tyre	28 Knife	42 Ron
01 Suit	15 Tail	29 Knob	43 Ram
02 Sun	16 Dish	30 Mouse	44 Rear
03 Sam	17 Dog	31 Matt	45 Roll
04 Sire	18 Dove	32 Mine	46 Rich
05 Sail	19 Tub	33 Mom	47 Rick
06 Sash	20 Nose	34 Mare	48 Rave
07 Sock	21 Knot	35 Mail	49 Rope
08 Safe	22 Nun	36 Mitch	50 Lace
09 Soup	23 Gnome	37 Mike	51 Light
10 Dice	24 Nora	38 Movie	52 Line
11 Tot	25 Nail	39 Mop	53 Lamb
12 Tin	26 Nash	40 Rose	54 Laura
13 Tom	27 Nick	41 Rod	55 Lily

56 Latch	67 Jock	78 Cuff	89 Vibe
57 Lock	68 Chef	79 Cop	90 Boss
58 Love	69 Ship	80 Face	91 Bat
59 Loop	70 Case	81 Fat	92 Pen
60 Shoes	71 Cat	82 Fan	93 Pam
61 Jet	72 Ken	83 Foam	94 Bear
62 Sean	73 Comb	84 Fire	95 Bell
63 Gem	74 Car	85 Val	96 Bush
64 Jar	75 Goal	86 Fish	97 Bike
65 Shell	76 Cash	87 Vick	98 Bev
66 Josh	77 Cake	88 Fave	99 Bob.

Enjoy using what you've learned in this chapter to develop your ability to remember numbers! Doing so will help you to accomplish things that you may have previously thought to be impossible. You will also really set yourself apart from your peers and will have a leg up on achieving much more success in your career and personal life!

6
From the Boardroom Back to the Classroom

To further your career, it's important to be able to quickly learn new processes, technologies, terminology, and more. You may even have to earn a new certification at some point. Whether you're an executive, entrepreneur, salesperson, or other type of business professional, your ability to learn will directly impact your ability to succeed. Knowledge truly is power, and knowledge is gained through learning.

So, if you are determined to become successful, you will undoubtedly in some way, shape, or form continually find yourself to be a student of sorts, whether it be through an in-house company training programme, reading books on your own, or actually back in a school classroom setting. This chapter will help you to apply everything that you've learned in previous chapters to various information types applicable to both school and work.

Let's dive right into some examples:

If studying Biology, you might need to remember that the function of the *endoplasmic reticulum* is to carry protein out of cells. How can you commit this to memory using the memory principles that you've learned so far? You'll want to once again visualize by turning what you want to remember into a simple image or series of memorable images. You will also want to involve as many additional senses as you can, and use your creativity and imagination to make what you are seeing and experiencing in your mind as crazy and unusual as possible.

In addition to those principles that you've already learned from previous chapters, you'll need something new called the "placeholder image". A *placeholder image* is something that you will temporarily visualize and use to represent the word or term that you're trying to memorize. You'll then later translate that *placeholder image* back into the word or term. Let's clarify this by continuing with the endoplasmic reticulum example.

The first step to committing the function of the endoplasmic reticulum to memory is to decide on your *placeholder image* for the endoplasmic reticulum. This could simply be an image of blood *plasma*. Your placeholder image will later just need to "remind" you in some way of the original term or word. Keep in mind that you would have heard the word endoplasmic reticulum many times in class or would have read it many times in the Biology book that you are studying. An image of *plasma* should be sufficient to remind you of the word endo*plasm*ic reticulum that you'll be familiar with from your studies.

Now that we've established the simple image of blood *plasma* as your placeholder image to call to mind endoplasmic reticulum, we can use that placeholder image to help you to commit the endoplasmic reticulum's function to memory. Again, the endoplasmic reticulum carries protein out of cells.

To commit this to memory using your placeholder image, you might imagine a giant pool of plasma (endoplasmic reticulum). Floating on top of the plasma is a big juicy steak (placeholder for protein). The steak is trapped by what look like jail cells (placeholder for cells). The plasma then floats or carries the steak right out of the jail cells. You end up with a very simple and memorable image of plasma floating a juicy steak out of jail cells! All that's left now is to simply translate that simple imagery with the placeholder images back into what the placeholders represent. So, what did you just see? You just saw the endoplasmic reticulum carry protein out of cells! This is an amazingly easy way to turn even very complex terminology into a simple series of memorable images.

Let's continue on with another and slightly different example. If studying Introductory Psychology, you will likely learn about Classical Conditioning. In class, you will probably read or hear about the experiment with Pavlov's dogs. During this experiment, researchers would bring out steak so that it could be seen by a group of dogs. Upon seeing the steak, the dogs would salivate at the sight of the steak. Later in the experiment, researchers would ring a bell when they brought out the steak to the dogs. Over time, the dogs became *conditioned* to salivate to the sound of the bell ringing even without any steak present. This type of conditioning is known as Classical Conditioning.

In Introductory Psychology, the concept of Operant Conditioning is usually also taught. An experiment to demonstrate Operant Conditioning has been done with rats and a maze. Researchers would put a rat in a maze, and if the rat takes the correct route to the right, nothing happens to it and it can get through the maze without any harm. If however, the rat takes the false route to the left, it will experience an electric shock. In this situation, the rat becomes *conditioned* over time to always go right so that it avoids the shock. This type of conditioning that involves experience as well as aspects of reward and punishment is known as Operant Conditioning.

Now, if being tested on an Introductory Psychology exam, a lot of students will mix up the terms Classical Conditioning and Operant Conditioning. They might write "operant" where they should write "classical", or vice versa. However, students who have developed the memory skills taught in this book might store in their mind an image of a dog salivating with a violin (placeholder for classical) in its mouth. That would lock into the student's mind that the experiment with the dogs salivating was the one that depicted *classical* conditioning.

I hope you're starting to see the various ways that you can creatively tweak what you are learning in this book to remember just about *anything* at all. If studying for an exam, I'd recommend combining what you learn about *placeholder images* in this chapter along with Journey Method. So, if you are to be tested on 50 new terms or concepts for an exam, you would store images along 50 locations of your journey. The first location of your journey might have the plasma carrying the juicy steak out of jail cells, and the second location of your journey might have the dog salivating with a violin in its mouth, and so on. I hope you're getting excited because soon no exam will be much of a challenge for you!

Let's go over another example so that you'll be even more comfortable when needing to tackle various concepts and terminology that you might encounter in your studies. In Physics, you'll learn and might need to remember that *convection* is the transfer of heat from an area of higher temperature to an area of lower temperature. In this case, I would use a "convention" as my placeholder image for "convection".

You can visualize this convention as consisting of two areas, an area upstairs with people above, and a lower area with people downstairs. A fire (placeholder for heat) breaks out upstairs and people start running away trying to escape from the fire. They run downstairs. The fire then transfers down to the lower area and people down below begin running from the fire trying to escape. You now have a very memorable image. What did you just see happen? You just witnessed the transfer of heat (fire) from an area of higher temperature (upstairs with the fire) to an area of lower temperature (downstairs that didn't at first have the fire). Once again, you've turned a complex term or concept into a simple series of memorable images using the idea of *placeholder images*. You'll note that this process not only improves your memory of the concept but also in many cases your understanding as well.

Let's move on to an example from Art History. The famous painting "The Scream" was painted by Münch. When pronounced properly, the name "Münch" sounds a lot like the word "monk". So we can use an image of a monk as our placeholder image for Münch. We can thus commit the information that "The Scream" was painted by Münch to memory by imagining that the ghost-like looking figure from that particular painting magically walks out of the painting. It then puts on a hood, and starts bowing and lighting candles as a monk might do. When you later need to recall who painted "The Scream", the image of the monk bowing and lighting candles will immediately return to your mind and remind you that it was painted by Münch. (Or perhaps an image of a monk screaming?)

One of my favourite examples is a hilarious one that comes from Geography. The capital of the country Bhutan is Thimpu. You can ensure that you remember this by picturing imagery of putting a "boot on" as your placeholder image for "Bhutan". Next, you can picture someone that you know named "Tim" going "poo" on the boot to remind you of "Thimpu". That memorable series of images is likely to stay firmly in your memory for a long while! (And will undoubtedly help in your future crossword puzzles!)

Since you've already memorized the top 20 countries in Europe by their GDP in a previous chapter, why not challenge yourself to use what you've just learned with the Bhutan example to memorize all of their capitals as well?

Let's approach a different type of exam situation. What if you were presented with a series of images in a Mathematics exam and asked to identify which one is in the shape of a *helix*? A helix is in fact shaped rather like a spring. You might imagine a spring that looks like the Slinky toy. This spring is covered in sores until the sores are made to disappear by a large tongue that gives it some "healing licks". The image of the "healing licks" is of course your placeholder image for "helix". When you are looking over the series of images in your exam, as soon as you see the shape that looks like a spring, the placeholder image of "healing licks" will immediately come back to your mind and you'll know that one is the helix!

In the financial services industry, what do the terms *bull market* and *bear market* mean? A bull market is a financial market in which stock prices are rising or expected to rise. A bear market is a financial market in which stock prices are falling or expected to fall. You can easily commit this to memory by picturing a "bull" (placeholder for bull market) pushing money up a hill so that it is "rising", and a "bear" (placeholder for bear market) pushing money down a hill so that it is "falling". With those images stored in your mind, it should be very easy to remember the meaning of the terms bull market and bear market!

Let's go over an example from Astronomy to illustrate how to tackle another type of term or definition. The point at which an object that is travelling around the Earth is at its farthest from the Earth is called the *apogee*. We could use an image of an apple with a "G"-shaped bite out of it to be our placeholder image for apogee. Now, visualize an object of some sort travelling around the Earth continuously. As the object travels around the Earth it is sometimes very close to it and at other times very far from it. Whenever the object is at its farthest from the Earth it instantly turns into the apple with the "G"-shaped bite out of it (placeholder for apogee). This will help you to remember that when an object circling the Earth is at its farthest from the Earth that particular point is called the apogee!

Let's say that at work you are presented with a chart that would be useful to commit to memory. The chart depicts the source of sales this past quarter and their corresponding percentages. 40% came from online marketing efforts, 30% came from word-of-mouth, 20% came from repeat customers, and 10% came from PR efforts. How can you commit this work-related information to memory using what you've learned so far in this book? You might visualize a computer connected to the internet (placeholder image for online marketing) and with multi-coloured roses (image for 40% based on the Phonetic Alphabet System covered in Chapter 5) coming out of it. Next, you can picture a giant mouth (placeholder image for word-of-mouth) with mice (image for 30%) running out of it. Visualize some people (placeholder image for customers) with really large noses (image for 20%) next. Lastly, picture a pile of newspapers and magazines (placeholder for PR) that have toes (image for 10%) wiggling all over them.

At this point, given any particular source of sales, you should be able to easily remember the corresponding percentage. When you think of "repeat customers", your placeholder image of the people will immediately come to mind, and you'll see them with the really large noses, so you'll know that the corresponding percentage is 20%. It's truly amazing what you are able to accomplish with just a little bit of memory training.

Let's now memorize the sources of sales in order from the highest percentage to the lowest. You could accomplish this with either the Journey Method or the Story Method. I'll go ahead and illustrate this process using the Story Method and your place-holder images. I'd like you to picture a computer that's connected to the internet (online sales). On the computer's screen, a giant mouth (word-of-mouth) appears and it starts to continuously open and close. A bunch of people (repeat customers) begin to walk out of the mouth. The people are reading newspapers and magazines (PR). Simply replay through the story in your mind and you'll be able to recall all of the sources of sales in order. From the imagery that you created earlier, you could also recall the corresponding percentages as well if you'd like.

Your company has just released a new product and as a member of the sales team you need to know all of the product's benefits and be able to talk about them with potential customers. In particular, you need to remember that this product offers the following benefits over its competitors: it's faster, it costs less, it provides more flexibility, it saves time, and it's easier to use. Let's handle this using the Journey Method.

You have five benefits to commit to memory, so you'll need a journey that consists of five different locations. Go ahead and choose five locations from your current place of work in an ordering that would make sense for you to traverse them just as you learned to do in Chapter 2. At the first location of your journey, you see a man running faster and faster (placeholder image for product benefit of being faster). At the second location of your journey, you find a large pile of money that just keeps shrinking into a smaller and smaller pile (placeholder image for product costing less).

Your journey's next location has a rubber rod that continuously wraps itself around the location in many different directions because of its incredible flexibility (placeholder image for product's flexibility). At your journey's next location, you see a Rolex watch jump into a safe (placeholder image for saves time). At the last location of your journey, you see a baby using the new product (placeholder image for easier to use)! Now, simply take a mental walk back through your journey and the images that you've placed at each location will easily remind you of all of the new product's benefits!

It's my hope that the examples given in this chapter have helped you to realize that the memory skills you are developing can be applied to learning just about anything at all! The ability to quickly learn new terminology, key points from research, information from charts, and new product information will give you an edge in any career. You are now well on your way to achieving greater business success!

7
Speak Your Client's Language

No matter what type of business you're in, at some point you may be doing business with people who speak another language. It's always pleasing to clients if you at least make an effort to learn some simple key words and phrases in their language. This can definitely help to establish more rapport with clients and can potentially even open up a whole new client base if you're able to develop sufficient foreign language skills. This short chapter will cover how to apply the memory techniques that you've learned so far to learning a foreign language.

One major part of learning a foreign language is to learn the rules of grammar in the language. Once you've learned the rules of grammar, you'll then be able to apply those rules to vocabulary in order to form sentences and phrases. Another part of learning a foreign language is to build your vocabulary in the language by learning as many new words as possible. What are the words for "man", "woman", "book", "computer", and so on? This vocabulary building part of learning a new language tends to be the most time consuming aspect for people.

Mastering your pronunciation is yet another element of learning a foreign language. You may be saying the correct word in a language and perhaps people that speak that language can understand what you're saying, but your pronunciation may be slightly off and have room for refinement.

Of the three parts of learning a new language that I just mentioned, the part that I can help you with the most using the memory techniques in this book that you've been learning is the vocabulary building. You can easily learn 100 new words a day if you are motivated and correctly apply the right memory improvement principles. I'm about to show you just how easy this can really be.

Let's get started by learning some new words in the Korean language. The Korean equivalent of the English word "bean" is "kong". This can be committed to memory by first visualizing a gigantic green "bean". You then see King "Kong" come along and he begins to chow down on the bean causing pieces of it to fly all over the place as he eats it. Later, when you need to recall the Korean word for "bean", the image of King "Kong" eating the bean will immediately return to your mind and you'll be able to recall that the word that you're looking for is "kong".

(I'd like to point out that the pror
Korean word "kong" does not sou
the "Kong" in King Kong. In fact,
netically more like "koh"+"ong". H(
mind that when you're studying a for
you'll likely be taking a class in whic
larly hear the instructor pronouncing tl
that you're trying to learn, and/or you
ing to CDs, and/or reading books. So, ir
the word "kong", if you had been studyi
you would have likely heard it many tin
and be familiar with how to pronounce i
Thus, an image of King Kong would be e
"remind" you of the word "kong" that yo
studying even though it is not pronounced ii
the same way.)

The imagery serves as a mental "cue" to he
call to mind the correct word that you're lc
for from among the many words that you ma)
encountered during your studies of the languaﾟ
the case of the word "bean", a single image of
Kong is enough to remind us of the word "koɪ
However, in other cases we may need a series
images to remind us sufficiently of the foreign lɑ
guage word. Let's move on to an example that w
illustrate this.

The Korean word for "water" is "mul". The worɑ
"mul" when spoken sounds sort of like "moo-l".
We can commit this to memory by imagining a giant
"pool" of water (placeholder imagery for water). A

w then jumps into the pool of water and starts
swim around, so it's no longer a "poo-l" of
ater but now a "moo-l" of water (placeholder
nagery for "mul")! When you later need to recall
he Korean word for "water", the imagery of the
ool of water that turns into a "moo-l" because of
he cow will come back to you and remind you to
say "mul".

The Korean word for "chicken" is "dalg", which
sounds sort of like "tack" when spoken. Picture a
chicken with a giant *tack* going through it. That will
help you to say "dalg" when you need to recall the
Korean word for "chicken".

"Ppang" is the Korean word for "bread". When
spoken it sounds similar to "bang" in English. Visualize a loaf of bread that fires off like a gun. When it
fires, a flag with the word "bang" on it pops out of
the bread as it would from a toy gun. This imagery
will cue you to say "ppang" when you need to say
"bread" in Korean.

The Korean word for "rice" is "bap". When spoken,
the Korean word "bap" sounds a lot like the English
word "pop". Imagine that you are eating a bowl of
rice (rice) and it starts to *pop* like popcorn (pop) and
hit you in the face. This will help you to say "bap"
when you need to say "rice" in Korean.

"Coffee" in Korean is "keopi", which sounds a
lot like the English word "copy" when spoken.

Imagine that you put a cup of *coffee* on a *copy* machine and hit the start button. This causes the machine to magically start spitting out real cups of coffee. This imagery will cue you to say "keopi" when you need to say "coffee" in Korean, because the imagery of the magic *copy* machine will come back to you when you think of *coffee*.

"House" in Korean is "jib". "Jib" when spoken sounds a lot like "jeep" in English, so I want you to picture that your *house* is being carted off on the back of a *jeep*. This will remind you that the Korean for "house" is "jib".

The Korean word for "sugar" is "seoltang", which sounds like "soul-tongue" when spoken. Visualize boxes and boxes of sugar. A ghost-like figure, a *soul*, rises out of the boxes and begins to stick out and wiggle its giant *tongue* (imagery to represent "soul"+"tongue"). When you later need to say "sugar" in Korean you'll remember the "soul"+"tongue" and that will cue you to say *seoltang*.

When memorizing foreign language vocabulary words using imagery as you've been learning to do in this chapter, it's wise to decide on images that will represent certain syllables that words may contain at the beginning, middle, or end. Apples could serve to remind you of the syllable "a", which sounds like "uh". I chose apples simply because the word "apples" begins with the letter "a". A hula hoop could serve to remind you of the syllable "o", which sounds like "oh". In this case, I chose a hula hoop because it has the same shape as an "o". As you can see, there are different ways to go about choosing your images, but they should always serve in some way to remind you of the syllable that you'll need to commit to memory.

Let me illustrate how your images for syllables can be very useful when studying foreign language vocabulary, by teaching you to remember a couple of words in Spanish. The Spanish word for "chair" is "silla", which sounds like "sea-uh" when spoken, because two "l's" in Spanish pronounces like a "y". I'd like you to picture a chair. This chair is floating in the sea and getting broken apart by the waves. As this is happening to the chair, apples are flying out of it. So when you need to say chair in Spanish, you'll think of the sea first (sea) and next the apples (uh) and will be able to say "silla".

"Tio" is the Spanish word for "uncle", and it sounds like "tea-oh" when spoken. You can commit this to memory by imagining your *uncle* drinking a cup of *tea* (tea) that has *hula hoops* (oh) coming out of it. This will help you to say "tio" when you need to say "uncle" in Spanish.

Let's quickly review the foreign language vocabulary words that we've covered, and then I'll show you a really cool benefit of going about studying new words with the methods taught in this chapter.

English Word	Foreign Word	Approx. Pronunciation	Imagery
bean	Kong	"koh-ong"	King Kong is eating a bean
water	Mul	"moo-l"	A cow swimming in a pool of water
chicken	Dalg	"tack"	A chicken with a giant tack going through it
bread	Ppang	"bang"	A loaf of bread fires a bang flag
rice	bap	"pop"	A bowl of rice starts to pop and hit your face
coffee	Keopi	"copy"	A copy machine starts to copy some coffee
house	Jib	"jeep"	Your house is being carted off by a jeep
sugar	seoltang	"soul-tongue"	A soul wiggling a tongue rises from sugar
chair	silla	"sea-uh"	A chair broken up by the sea with apples flying
uncle	tio	"tea-oh"	Uncle drinking cup of tea with hula hoops

Review the chart above once or twice and then try to complete the following chart:

Foreign Word	English Word
kong	
mul	
dalg	
ppang	
bap	
keopi	
jib	
seoltang	
silla	
tio	

You'll find that you're easily able to come up with the corresponding word in English for any of the foreign language words, just as you were the other way around, because your images are intertwined. This is a very nice benefit to studying foreign language vocabulary with the methods covered in this chapter. When you hear a speaker saying one of the foreign language words that you've studied, you're likely to easily understand what is being said because you'll know the English equivalent thanks to your imagery.

Using the technique that you've learned in this chapter probably won't be enough to become fluent in a foreign language. However, it will definitely help you to quickly build up your vocabulary in a new language, and that can be very useful. Just making an effort to learn some key words in a language spoken by your clients and colleagues will impress them. People really appreciate any efforts made to learn their language, so it definitely helps to build rapport. This could also very well help you to get along better on a business trip to another country. Keep in mind that if you were in Korea, you wouldn't necessarily have to say "Can I get some sugar, please?" if you needed some for your coffee. It would probably be effective enough to simply say "seoltang?" in an inquisitive tone! You'll get your sugar and I promise you the waiter will smile and be impressed. So will your associates dining with you!

But remember: it takes *study* and it takes *practice*!

Now, get out there and have fun learning some new words in another language!

8
All Work and No Play?

"**A**ll work and no play" is never a good idea! Thus far I've only taught you *business* applications for the memory skills that you're developing. In this chapter, I'd like to cover a *fun* application of memory skills that is of interest to many people. I'm going to teach you how to memorize playing cards! Why would I cover this in a business book? It's because the purpose of this book is to help you to develop memory skills that you can apply to become more successful in business.

Developing and sharpening any skill requires regular practice, and you'll be encouraged to practice if it's easy and fun for you. One of the easiest ways to practice and really sharpen your memory skills is to memorize decks of playing cards. Once you know how to memorize a deck of playing cards, it's a simple matter to take out a deck, shuffle it up, and then commit it to memory. In order to memorize a playing card deck, you'll need to apply many of the same principles and techniques that you learned earlier for business purposes. Thus, memorizing playing cards regularly will definitely improve your ability to remember names, numbers, speeches, terminology, languages, and more!

The first thing you'll need to become an expert card player is to turn each playing card into an image. You can do this using the Phonetic Alphabet System that you learned earlier in Chapter 5. Using that system, playing cards can be turned into words. Those words will allow you to produce in your mind corresponding images. Let me start with a specific playing card as an example to illustrate exactly how this works.

The word I use for the Ace of Spades is *seat*. How did I come up with *seat* for the Ace of Spades? The word for a specific playing card will begin with the same consonant letter/sound as its suit. In this case, the suit is Spades, which begins with the letter/sound "s", so our word must begin with an "s". The word for a specific playing card will end with a consonant sound, based on the Phonetic Alphabet System, that corresponds to the *rank* of the playing card. An "Ace" has the rank of "1", so our word must end with the "t" or "d" sound, since those are the sounds that correspond to the number "1" in the Phonetic Alphabet System.

As was the case for number sequences, vowel sounds can be inserted anywhere to help you form a word for a playing card. So, I inserted the "ea" and came up with the word "seat". Again, the "s" in seat came from "Spades" and the "t" in seat came from the Ace's rank of "1". My word for the 2 of

Spades is *sun*. The "s" in sun came from "Spades" and the "n" in sun came from the rank of "2". Study the following (playing card)/(word) pairs and make sure that you understand them before you proceed with this chapter:

3 of Spades = Sam
4 of Spades = sore
5 of Spades = sail
6 of Spades = sash
7 of Spades = sock
8 of Spades = safe
9 of Spades = soup

For cards with the rank of "10" we will only use the "0" from 10 and ignore the "1", so words corresponding to cards of rank "10" should end with the "s" or "z" sound, which correspond to "0" in the Phonetic Alphabet System. Thus, the word for the 10 of Spades is *sauce*. The words corresponding to the Jacks in a deck will always be the same as the suit for that particular Jack. Thus, the word for the Jack of Spades is simply *spade*.

For the Queens and Kings in a deck, we'll use Queens and Kings from history or pop culture that we can in some way associate with the corresponding suit. For the Queen and King of Spades, we'll use colour association. The suit of Spades is black in colour, so we'll use a *Queen Bee* for the Queen of Spades, since a Queen Bee is covered in black bands. We'll use *King Kong* for the King of Spades, since King Kong's fur is black.

Here is a complete list of playing cards in a standard 52-card deck and my corresponding words:

Ace of **Spades** = seat	Ace of **Hearts** = hat

2 of Spades = sun	2 of Hearts = hen
3 of Spades = sam	3 of Hearts = ham
4 of Spades = sore	4 of Hearts = hair
5 of Spades = sail	5 of Hearts = hail
6 of Spades = sash	6 of Hearts = hash
7 of Spades = sock	7 of Hearts = hook
8 of Spades = safe	8 of Hearts = hoof
9 of Spades = soup	9 of Hearts = hoop
10 of Spades = sauce	10 of Hearts = house
Jack of Spades = spade	Jack of Hearts = heart
Queen of Spades = Queen Bee	Queen of Hearts = Dairy Queen (might be unhealthy for heart)
King of Spades = King Kong	King of Hearts = Burger King (might be unhealthy for heart)
Ace of **Diamonds** = dad	Ace of **Clubs** = cat
2 of Diamonds = dan	2 of Clubs = can
3 of Diamonds = dime	3 of Clubs = cam
4 of Diamonds = door	4 of Clubs = car
5 of Diamonds = doll	5 of Clubs = coal
6 of Diamonds = dish	6 of Clubs = cash
7 of Diamonds = duck	7 of Clubs = cake
8 of Diamonds = dove	8 of Clubs = cuff
9 of Diamonds = dip	9 of Clubs = cop
10 of Diamonds = dice	10 of Clubs = case
Jack of Diamonds = diamond	Jack of Clubs = club
Queen of Diamonds = Queen Elizabeth	Queen of Clubs = Queen Latifah
King of Diamonds = King Tut	King of Clubs = Michael Jackson

Review the pairs above. Feel free to change any of the words for playing cards if you feel that another word will work better for you personally for any particular card. However, once you decide on a word, I advise that you never change it. Keep in mind that in the end, what's important are the *images*, not the words. You'll first learn the *words* for the playing cards, but the end goal is for you to instantly have a specific *image* pop into your head when you see its corresponding playing card. The only way to reach that level of fluency is to make sure that you see the same image in your head for a playing card every time. Once you have a fair working knowledge of your images for each card, you can move on to memorizing an entire deck in order!

Assuming that you know your images for each playing card fairly well, the next step will be for you to come up with a 26-location journey. You learned the Journey Method in Chapter 2. You'll be using a 26-location journey so that you can place two card images at each location in order to store a 52 (2 × 26) card deck in your memory. Let's say that the first card in a deck that you're trying to memorize is the King of Spades. You might imagine in this case an image of King Kong (image for King of Spades) at the first location of your journey.

I advise putting two card images at each journey location, so if the second card in the deck is the 4 of Clubs (car), you might see King Kong eating a car at the first location of your journey. This would tell you that the first two cards in the deck are the King

117

of Spades (King Kong) followed by the 4 of Clubs (car). If the next two cards in the deck are the Ace of Clubs followed by the 10 of Diamonds, you might see a *cat* rolling *dice* at the second location of your journey. Continue along like this placing two card images at the remaining locations of your journey for every two cards and you will have memorized the entire deck!

I strongly encourage you to study this chapter well, so that you can start to regularly memorize decks of playing cards. Even memorizing only a half deck of 26 cards (two images at each of 13 locations) on a regular basis will serve to sharpen the memory skills that you need for an edge in business. The more you practise, the faster you're going to get, so memorizing decks will take less and less time. Before you know it, you'll be able to memorize a 52-card deck in minutes!

Make a game of it as you practise. Play it with a friend or a business associate. The main thing is to *have fun*!

9
Final Considerations

In this chapter, I'd like to give you some additional tips and considerations to help you turn your memory into a powerful business tool. Specifically, I want to give you some tips for refining what you've learned so far and for combining it all with other important learning principles, as well as some of my thoughts on diet and exercise as they relate to memory. If you've been studying and *practising*, you've already started to develop incredible memory skills. This short chapter will serve to make your skills even stronger.

Earlier in this book, you learned to take whatever it is that you want to remember and turn it into a simple image or series of images. You've also learned to add as many additional senses to your imagery as possible to activate more areas of your brain and make things even more memorable. In addition, you learned to make what you're experiencing in your mind crazy, unusual, and out of the ordinary. Always keeping those three principles in mind as you commit information to memory will help you tremendously.

The more you practice, the faster you will become at creating your images. Also, with practice you'll be able to see the imagery in your mind more clearly. As you continue to practise and develop your memory skills, you'll start to discover what types of images work best for you personally. However, it might be useful to experiment with and try out the following tips:

- Make your images larger than life. You might have noticed that in many of the examples I've given you, I described items as being *giant* or *gigantic*. This is because it's an effective way to make your imagery extraordinary. A gigantic duck the size of Godzilla is much more memorable than just an ordinary duck!

- Visualize tens, hundreds, or thousands of an object rather than just a single object by itself. What's more memorable, a ball hitting a window, or thousands of balls hitting a window?

- Make the colour of your images different from what you'd expect to see in real life. A yellow banana is not nearly as memorable as a purple or rainbow coloured banana!

- Use lots of action in your imagery! A person just standing on a bed is not as memorable as a person continuously jumping up and down on the bed and doing backflips as if on a trampoline.

- Imagine objects doing things they wouldn't normally be able to do in real life. Seeing a pair of scissors cut a piece of paper isn't particularly memorable. However, seeing a pair of scissors somehow cut up a TV set into pieces would be extremely memorable!

Everything you've been learning in this book will help improve your ability to remember, but how long will you retain the information? Using the techniques I've been teaching you will automatically keep the information in your mind much longer than it would remain otherwise, because with these techniques you are using much more of your brain to encode the information. However, you will eventually forget much of what you are committing to memory if you don't review it.

Studies have shown that one of the best ways to commit information to long-term memory is with *spaced repetition*. Spaced repetition involves spacing out or increasing the time intervals between your reviews. The idea is to ideally review the information just before you are about to forget it. Using the memory techniques covered in this book together with spaced repetition is a powerful combination that is incredibly effective for committing information to long-term memory. For information you want or need to remember long-term, I recommend the following series of spaced reviews that has served me well over the years:

- The first review should come just before you go to sleep on the same day that you start to learn the information. This is because many studies have shown that if you review something just before you go to sleep, your brain will actually process and *solidify* that information in your mind overnight and your recall of it will significantly improve. One theory as to why this works is that by reviewing just before sleep, you are in a way instructing your brain as to what information to consolidate.

- I like to do a second review sometime early the next morning. Maybe while eating breakfast or taking a shower, you can quickly run through your imagery.

- I recommend for the third review to come about one week later. If you've done the first two reviews, you'll likely still remember the information after one week but may be just about to forget it.

- The fourth review I recommend coming about two weeks after the third review.

- I usually do a fifth and final review about four weeks after my fourth review. At this point, the information is usually in my long-term memory and I will be able to recall it even many months later. Of course, if I review it months later, I will retain the information even longer.

The review I've outlined above has worked well for me and it incorporates the well-studied concept of spaced repetition. However, it's best to just consider it a rough guideline. The most effective series of reviews for long-term memory will depend on the individual, and also on what exactly it is you are trying to memorize. It's a good idea to start with the outline I've provided and then tweak it to meet your specific needs.

Another important principle to apply in conjunction with the memory techniques you've been learning in this book is that of *active recall*. Active recall simply involves practising retrieving the information you've committed to memory. This is opposed to reviewing the information over and over again without ever making an attempt to recall it. Performing self-tests while studying is a great way to engage in active recall. Earlier, you learned the top 20 countries in Europe in order by their GDP. Simply reading the list over and over again, and even just reviewing your images over and over without testing yourself on the recall, would be considered merely *passive reviewing*. However, asking yourself what the #7 ranked country is and answering that question, or challenging yourself to list all 20 countries in order, would be considered *active* recall.

If you really want to consolidate information into long-term memory, it would be ideal to use the techniques you learned in earlier chapters to memorize the information and also be sure to test yourself on recalling it. It's not nearly as effective to simply review your imagery multiple times without making attempts to recall the information that you're trying to commit to memory.

Your diet is something else important to consider if you're serious about improving your ability to remember things. B-vitamins are important for mental energy and concentration, so if you're not getting them from food, I'd recommend a B-vitamin complex supplement. Omega-3 fatty acids are essential for normal brain function, so if you aren't eating a lot of fish or other food rich in them, it will likely benefit you to take fish oil or another Omega-3 supplement. In addition to the specific nutrients just mentioned, it's important to keep in mind that it's widely acknowledged that a healthy body equals a healthy mind. So, in addition to B-vitamins and Omega-3s, if you aren't getting other essential vitamins and minerals that your body needs to function properly, it will inevitably have a negative impact on your memory.

It's best to get the nutrients that your body needs from natural food sources, but if you don't have the healthiest diet, it might be a good idea to take a daily multivitamin to at least try to compensate for what your diet may be lacking. Gingko Biloba is a herb that has been shown in some studies to promote learning and memory. Some research has concluded that it's very beneficial, whereas other research says not so much. I have personally taken Ginkgo Biloba and recommend it, but it's a good idea to do your own research and consult your doctor before you start to take it.

Regular exercise is another consideration when trying to improve your memory and keep it sharp. We all know that exercise is important to keeping our bodies healthy, and thus it's important for our minds and memory. Specifically, regular exercise increases blood flow to the brain, and this means more oxygen and energy, which improves brain performance. It doesn't take much! Even taking short walks just a few times per week can have a positive impact on your brain.

So, I guess I should say, "Remember to exercise if you want to remember!"

10
This IS a Test

Congratulations on making it to the final chapter! If you've reached this point, it means you have already developed some powerful memory skills that are going to help you become much more successful in business. The exercises in this chapter are going to develop your skills further while at the same time demonstrating just how much you've already learned. My hope is that you'll find these exercises to be both challenging and fun!

Let's start with something relatively simple. Using the Story Method, please commit to memory the following random list of words:

disk
camera
flamingo
pizza
raccoon
table
television

hat
painting
suitcase
blanket
cabinet
bench
grass
planet
circle
water
salsa
book
elf

Test your recall by filling in the blanks on this page:

_____	_____
_____	_____
_____	_____
_____	_____
_____	_____
_____	_____
_____	_____
_____	_____
_____	_____
_____	_____
_____	_____
_____	_____
_____	_____
_____	_____
_____	_____
_____	_____
_____	_____
_____	_____
_____	_____
_____	_____
_____	_____
_____	_____
_____	_____
_____	_____
_____	_____
_____	_____
_____	_____
_____	_____

Let's try a similar exercise using the Story Method. This time you'll once again memorize a random list of words, but the words will be more abstract instead of simple nouns. In order to pull this off, you'll simply need to come up with images that will in some way *remind* you of each word as you build your story. Here's the new list:

age
destiny
constant
verify
commit
intelligence
exercise
clarify
time
stubborn
diligence
ego
duration
entertain
valuable
beauty
rest
investment
cancel
love

Test your recall by filling in the blanks on this page:

_____   _____

_____   _____

_____   _____

_____   _____

_____   _____

_____   _____

_____   _____

_____   _____

_____   _____

_____   _____

_____   _____

_____   _____

_____   _____

_____   _____

_____   _____

_____   _____

_____   _____

_____   _____

_____   _____

_____   _____

_____   _____

_____   _____

_____   _____

_____   _____

I'd now like you to memorize 20 random names of people instead of 20 random words. Please use the Story Method. This will be great practice in coming up with images to remind you of people's names! Here's the list:

Tom
Edward
Nancy
Clare
Elizabeth
John
Timothy
Oscar
Dennis
James
Daisy
Crystal
Harry
Angela
Jessica
Emily
Donald
Pamela

Test your recall by filling in the blanks on this page:

_____	_____
_____	_____
_____	_____
_____	_____
_____	_____

Let's try a similar exercise using the Story Method to memorize a random list of names. This time, however, the names will not be common English names. In order to pull this off, you'll simply need to come up with an image or series of images to remind you of each name as you build your story. It may be necessary to break certain names down by syllable. The name Bijal might be remembered by imagining a bee (Bi-) covered in gel (jal). Here's the new list:

Bijal

Revaldo

Torun

Mena

Dhaka

Nikola

Iryna

Henning

Aguta

Lenka

Amrut

Somia

Sterling

Roberto

Masayuki

Jacco

Chen

Aksel

Bendt

Banu

Test your recall by filling in the blanks on this page:

_____	_____
_____	_____
_____	_____
_____	_____
_____	_____
_____	_____
_____	_____
_____	_____
_____	_____
_____	_____
_____	_____
_____	_____
_____	_____
_____	_____
_____	_____
_____	_____
_____	_____
_____	_____
_____	_____
_____	_____
_____	_____
_____	_____
_____	_____
_____	_____
_____	_____
_____	_____
_____	_____
_____	_____

Next, you'll use the Journey Method to memorize a list of random words. There will be 20 words, so you'll need a 20-location journey. Here's the list:

pizza
crayon
panda
diaper
emerald
feather
casino
basket
salad
disco
zebra
cottage
flower
island
coffee
tent
ocean
pillow
suit
candle

Test your recall by filling in the blanks on this page:

_____	_____
_____	_____
_____	_____
_____	_____
_____	_____
_____	_____
_____	_____
_____	_____
_____	_____
_____	_____
_____	_____
_____	_____
_____	_____
_____	_____
_____	_____
_____	_____
_____	_____
_____	_____
_____	_____
_____	_____
_____	_____
_____	_____
_____	_____
_____	_____

You are going to need a 12-location journey for the next challenge. I'd like you to commit to memory 12 simple points of a short presentation about the 2008 United States Presidential election. It doesn't matter if you have no interest in American politics. This exercise is simply to practise and test yourself on committing to memory a speech or presentation. "Remember", as discussed in Chapter 4, you only need a simple image or series of images to help remind you of each point. An image of Obama and McCain boxing each other would remind you to say, "Who will win, Obama or McCain?" An image of McCain racing on a donkey (Democrat mascot) and badly losing the race would remind you to say, "Democrats think that McCain can't win". Here are the 12 simple points of the presentation:

I. Who will win, Obama or McCain?
II. Democrats think that McCain can't win
   a) Republic brand is shot, so Republican candidate cannot win
   b) A McCain win would represent a 3rd term for Bush, and no one wants this
   c) McCain is too old and would be the oldest President to ever take office
III. Republicans think that Obama can't win
   a) Lost ground in the primaries by losing a string of primaries to Clinton
   b) Close Obama and Clinton race has divided the Democrat party
   c) Obama lacks support from White working class

IV. I don't know who will win; however:
   a) For McCain to win, he must separate himself from Bush and typical Republicans
   b) For Obama to win, he must gain support of voters from White working class

Test your recall by filling out the outline below. You don't need to write out the points exactly as they appear above, but you must get the gist of each point across in the correct order.

  I.
  II.
    a)
    b)
    c)
 III.
    a)
    b)
    c)
 IV.
    a)
    b)

Next up is a fun test that will help sharpen your ability to use the Phonetic Alphabet System from Chapter 5 for remembering information that contains numbers. I'll give you a count for various random objects. For instance, 15 cameras. That could be memorized by simply picturing a camera sprouting a giant tail (15). Here we go:

15 cameras
25 tables
99 dogs
45 frisbees
11 hats
57 dragons
65 men
38 pens
30 shoes
27 women
95 castles
62 ghosts
18 cards
74 steaks
49 phones
41 keys
70 socks
68 penguins
42 eggs
90 bottles

Test your recall by filling in the blanks on this page:

90———————	25———————
41———————	42———————
11———————	57———————
65———————	30———————
38———————	27———————
95———————	62———————
18———————	70———————
68———————	99———————
74———————	49———————
45———————	15———————

I hope you've enjoyed the exercises in this final chapter and that they've helped you to realize just how much you've learned. You spent good money to buy this book and you've invested the time to read it. This means you have the desire to improve your memory and increase your success in the business world. In turn, you appreciate the value of *practice*!

You now have some incredibly useful memory skills that will benefit you throughout your career. Your newfound ability to remember *anything* you set your mind to will give you a tremendous advantage in all your endeavours. You've taken the time to hone your most important business asset and thus have come to wield a powerful weapon.

Now, get out there and conquer the business world!

About the Author

Chester Santos, "The International Man of Memory", has left an impression on all corners of the earth. Through his ability to demonstrate extraordinary feats of the mind, as well as educate others to do the same, this **U.S. Memory Champion** is widely regarded to be one of the greatest memory experts in the world. He has helped thousands of people to realize the benefits of an improved memory and sharper mind, and has appeared in the *New York*

Times, Wall Street Journal, San Francisco Chronicle, Washington Post, USA Today, PBS, CNN, and various other television, radio, and print media all over the world.

Through workshops, corporate training seminars, and his renowned speeches and presentations, Chester has developed a knack for passing on valuable memory techniques in ways that are easy to understand and retain for years to come. He has been a speaker for executive organizations such as YPO, CEO Clubs International, and AceTech as well as for many Fortune 500 companies, and prestigious universities including: the Royal University for Women in Bahrain, the Haas Graduate School of Business in Berkeley, Stanford University, and Harvard University. His iPhone application was featured by Apple and became an instant worldwide bestseller.

Acknowledgements

I'd like to express my thanks and appreciation to my mother Roxanne for always supporting my endeavours; to my friend and business mentor Mike Faith for all of his help and valuable advice over the years; to my friend and client Cash Nickerson for inspiring me with his success in so many areas; to my friend Harry Villegas for his years of moral support and for being a great sounding board; to my friend and client Ron Mallia for inspiring me with his business acumen and achievements; to my personal trainer Giana Lando for helping to keep my body in shape while I work my mind; to the brilliant and incredible Ed Addeo for all of his invaluable help getting this book out; to my super literary agent Bob Diforio for his help with my various works; and to the amazing team at Wiley for all of their hard work and for believing in this project.

Index